MW01644897

Lifting The Mask

A Path Away from Pressure and Towards Joy

SUZY DOMENICK

Edited by Laura Lindsey

DEDICATION

This book is dedicated to my mom, Honey. She has been the driving force for me to heal, grow and transform as I have helped to heal her as well. She showed me the power of female relationships and having women surrounding you. Her wisdom and love enabled me to see who I was and who I wanted to be.

ACKNOWLEDGMENTS

To write a book this personal and share my journey, I needed support and love all around me.

Thank you to my family who has stood by me through all the trials and tribulations of my life. I am so very blessed to have you all.

Thank you to my first writing coach, Susan, who helped me understand my gift of storytelling and gave me confidence in my writing.

Thank you to Gina, my first coach and spiritual advisor. Your wisdom and love continue to inspire me.

Thank you to my coaches Allyson and Laura, without your guidance, support, love and care, this book would have never gotten done.

Thank you to my writing buddy, Liz. You push me to be better every day. You're a force and I am so glad I can call you my friend.

Thank you to the women, my tribe, who have lifted me when down, held me when sad and loved me through it all. You are my sustenance.

"It took many years of vomiting up all the filth I'd been taught about myself, and half-believed, before I was able to walk on this earth as though I had a right to be here." - James Baldwin

CONTENTS

Introduction 1

Chapter 1 9

Chapter 2 23

Chapter 3 41

Chapter 4 53

Chapter 5 67

Chapter 6 75

Chapter 7 85

Chapter 8 99

Chapter 9 109

Final Reflections 131

INTRODUCTION

By society's definition, I had tremendous success by the time I was forty years old. I had a career as an executive in a Fortune 500 company making good money that also came with a lot of prestige. I owned a beautiful home with a pool, and was in love with my husband who seemed to love me as well. His two sons allowed me to flex my maternal muscles. I finally had the family I wanted. Yet, I was miserable. I was always feeling as if I couldn't catch up to others, I wasn't good enough. I was afraid someone would find out I really wasn't that smart or that good at what I did. I was filled with self-loathing, constantly critiquing myself and my body. My tendency was to try to control everything around me so it would go the way I wanted, exactly the way I wanted. I tried to control what my husband wanted, or did or even said. I tried to control everything at my job. I tried to control every part of my life.

Nothing I did was good enough in my eyes. When you fast forward to today, to the Suzy who is writing this book, those feelings no longer haunt me. I know I am worthy. I know I deserve the things I desire. I know I am enough. I release control. And I love myself, finally. Maybe for the first time in my life, I actually love all of me. I know many of us question ourselves, question our abilities, question our motives, question our behavior and most of all, we question our desires. How often do you say to yourself, "Who am I to do this?" The women I work with all have a few things very much in common; a lack of self-trust, self-love, and self-acceptance. They give everything to everyone else, and struggle with giving themselves what they need and want. They have literally lost themselves. They always ask me to fix them. I get to help them see they do not need fixing. Nobody is broken!

I want you to know you don't have to face everything by yourself. You, the woman who does for everyone and holds it together, all while crumbling on the inside, are not alone. You, the woman who is seen as independent and strong because you had no choice, and now asking for help feels like a weakness, can live differently. You, the woman who questions and judges yourself and doesn't feel worthy of what you have or what you desire, so you over compensate , and over-think...you can experience ease . You, the woman who believes she is a perfectionist, only to realize that she is afraid of failure and is disguising it with high standards, can thrive without unnecessary pressure. My hope as you read this is that you come to know you are worthy because you are alive. You have been conditioned to believe things about yourself that are not the truth. What I know for sure is there is a path to becoming the best, most authentic version of you and it begins with awareness and honesty. It takes becoming super vulnerable with yourself, and deeply examining your behaviors, your actions and your inactions with love, grace, and compassion. There is a path toward joy.

Much of my story is wrapped in my mom and my grandma's story. Each was an independent woman and ahead of their time. My mom was a driving force in raising me as an independent woman, teaching me to never need anything from anyone; hyperindependent, if you will. She wanted me to be everything she believed she was not. My grandmother was strength personified. She was also very resilient, with an amazing sense of humor. My mom and her sister taught me the power of female relationships, sisterhood and your tribe. Mom had lifelong friends. She always had women around her, including cousins who were raised more like siblings. Through watching her as well as being part of her tribe, I learned the value, love and depth that the sisterhood can give to us. That tribe, that group of women, sustains us.

As I have healed over the years, I understand both of them more and more, and appreciate the feminist views that shaped me. Mom and I had our bumps over the years, especially during my teen years and then again after my first divorce. Mom projected her fears, her scarcity mindset and her body images so much so they became one-hundred percent mine.

As an adult, I became increasingly close with my mom and her sister. We spent a lot of time together going to Atlantic City, going to see shows in the city, and spending time playing cards. The two of them were a hoot. My brother and I coined the term "the pigeon sisters" based on the flighty British sisters on the 70's sitcom *The Odd Couple*. When I was in college, my roommates looked forward to Honey and Kit stories. Like the time they showed up at a strange woman's house to attend a baby shower for their hairdresser, but they arrived a week early! Or when they used the bathroom on a plane together!

I enjoyed talking to them, laughing with them, and watching sports with them. One afternoon in 2015 we were out shopping for dresses for an upcoming wedding. We were chatting up a storm in the car when I asked a simple question to see what their response would be. There they both were, in their nineties looking back at life, and I knew they could pass along some wisdom.

"If you could write a letter to your younger self, what would you tell her?" I asked, directing the question to both of them.

"I would tell myself to manage my anger better and temper and watch the words that come out of my mouth. They are very hurtful and

I don't ever mean them!" My mom barely took a breath before answering me. She didn't even think about it, it was her first instinct. She quickly added, "And I would have learned more." The look on her face was pensive, and I was curious.

"What do you mean?" I asked.

"I was never as smart as Aunt Kit and I wanted to be. I could have applied myself more, stayed in college. I should have learned more." I realized at that moment that I was a lot like my mom. She compared herself to her sister, and I compared myself to every woman I knew. We both thought we weren't smart enough, pretty enough, thin enough, nice enough. We weren't enough. The realization that the wounds of my mother were also mine was eye opening for both of us. We shared a lot with each other over time; our disappointments, our deepest secrets. Telling her my deepest secrets was the beginning of my true healing.

My mom passed away in September of 2017. She was ninety-five years old. Of all the losses I have experienced, losing my mom has been the biggest, most traumatic of them all. She is the person I want to call every day, especially when I need someone to hear me. It didn't matter that she was ninety-five, I wanted her to live forever. I met with a medium not long after my mom died. She only knew my name and that I wanted to connect with my mom. A number of different people came through; cousins, and friends' parents, my brother, and then, finally, the medium asked me the question I'd been waiting for.

"Who is Honey?"

"That's Mom," I answered, smiling.

"Well she is coming through loud and clear!"

"That sounds about right," I confirmed, still smiling,

"What is happening in 2018? Early in the year."

"I am retiring from my career, and actually I recently decided to enroll in a coaching school. I want to do something fabulous in my retirement, I'm not done making my impact."

"Your mom is showing me fireworks and confetti, a confirmation that you are following the right path, and she is so happy for you."

"I feel her all the time," I confirmed with tears in my eyes. "I miss her everyday."

"Well," the medium said, "just know that she is celebrating you and affirms to me that your impact will be substantial."Things like this come up every time I am with a medium.

A few months ago, at another medium gallery, Mom came through. This time, the medium looked at me and said, "you are a cycle breaker. She wants you to know that is what you are doing." Validating for me what I believed, as I heal, she is healing. She continues to encourage my growth. I feel her and I receive a lot of signs from the Universe. Even as I started to write this book, I received signs of confirmation and affirmation from her all over the place. Her chosen method of signs is through butterflies because she knows how much I love them.

From the time I was in middle school I have loved butterflies. I initially just loved the colors and variations as well as the way they flitted around. I had butterfly pictures on my wall in my bedroom throughout my childhood and to this day. I would receive butterfly jewelry often from my parents and friends. The butterfly's transformation became more of a symbol for me as I grew older. I started to notice that butterflies showed up when I needed a sign that I was on the right path, or that an ancestor was nearby. My grandmother, Stella, was the first to show up for me as a butterfly. I remember it well. My first marriage was ending and I was thinking about her. I wanted her strength to help be okay. She was the strongest person I ever knew. Her strength was quiet, loving, and filled with conviction. Although on the outside I appeared tough and angry, the inner dialogue was completely different.

I remember wondering if I would ever be loved again. *Why am I the one of my friends whose marriage ended? Is it because I am such a bad person?* I was sitting on the patio of my condominium. It was the beginning of spring, only a few weeks after he and I finally split up for good. I had just placed some flowers in a pot on the patio. I sat there and began to cry. I began to speak to the flowers I had just planted. "Oh Grandma, why is this happening to me? Please help me be okay. Please let me know that everything will be okay." A few moments later, a beautiful monarch butterfly flitted by and stopped to enjoy one of the flowers. I immediately knew she heard me. She was there with me. I could feel her presence, her essence. I felt something and believed it was her. I knew then that I would survive this new journey, perhaps even thrive.

Another powerful moment when a butterfly showed up to assure me was in 2016. I had an unusual finding on a mammogram and my doctor sent me to a breast specialist. I made the decision not to tell anyone in my family. I decided if it was cancer, I would go through it without my parents or anyone else knowing except for the few friends closest to me. The specialist sent me for an ultrasound-guided needle biopsy. After the biopsy, I had to wait up to five days for results. That waiting was truly torture. All through that time, my mind was fucking with me. *If it's cancer, I will just get a boob job. I wished myself dead a number of times, maybe this time it will happen. Nobody will care if I die.* It was day five of waiting for results, and I was freaking out internally. I was sitting at my desk in my fourth-floor office in Connecticut, and I heard something bumping into one of the two walls of windows. I saw a beautiful yellow butterfly flying back and forth from one wall of windows to the other quickly. Just then, my cell phone rang and it was the doctor's office. My heart was beating out of my chest. I heard my doctor's voice telling me that there was no cancer detected, it was a benign cyst. I looked over at the butterfly still flying outside of my office, and I took a huge breath.

I called my cousin immediately to tell her the good news as well as the butterfly story. She is a gifted intuitive healer, and she had gotten a message from my deceased brother as I was receiving the phone call. She already knew everything was okay with me. The power of that yellow butterfly, and its insistence to get my attention, solidified for me that signs are a real thing. They are a real way to understand, validate, or change your path. It took time for me to truly trust my intuition, my inner wisdom, and the power of a sign, but once I allowed that trust, it changed everything. Signs have helped me a lot over my healing and transformation journey. Butterflies have been a very big part of those signs. And, of course, there were signs and validation along the journey of writing this book.

Writing a book this personal brings a lot of resistance with it. Sharing so much of myself and my story feels at times as if I am stark naked standing on the fifty-yard line of Giants Stadium. There is no more hiding. There is no more keeping things to myself that need to come out. Speaking your truth is not always an easy thing, hence the quote, "Speak your truth even if your voice shakes." During the process of writing this, I spent time on a retreat with other writers and healers, and our goal while we were there was to remove this resistance and move our story forward. My business coach, Allyson, is also a Reiki master and offered some healing as we ended our week together. During my Reiki session, my mom was with me. Her energy was strong and her voice even stronger. "Speak your truth," she said, over and over. As the Reiki session ended, I looked out into the garden to see a huge, yellow butterfly flying nearby. I took a huge breath, knowing I was on the right path and receiving my mom's affirmation. This book is my truth, my perspective, and my healing.

This is the story of me presenting as a lion when I was actually a feral kitten, to becoming a loving, whole being all of the time, authentically. This is a story of a woman who grew up in what was considered a normal, functional family with love around her, and yet she never thought she was lovable. This story is my perspective. You will notice that I do not give names in some cases. They are not important, but the lessons I learned are worth sharing. My hope is that you, my sister, see that you are not alone. You are not what you have believed you are; you are whoever you want to be or become. My wish is that my story inspires you to consider your own healing. My greatest message here is that all the suffering is not about you. It is about traumas and wounds that create stories and narratives that keep you believing you are small, and that you aren't enough. You can heal, grow, and transform your life. You can love and accept yourself fully, just like I learned to love and accept myself. I'm not promising an easy journey, but if you commit to finishing this book you will feel less alone, and more capable of taking control of your life. Moving away from pressure and towards joy. Let's begin

CHAPTER 1

Some people don't know they are at their breaking point until they are in the midst of it, and I was one of those people. Looking at a picture of me and my life, you would have thought I had it all. I was in my second marriage that many envied, he seemed so supportive and wonderful. I remember one New Year's Eve listening to two friends talking about how they needed to "find a guy like that," because he seemed like such a catch. I had a successful career as a senior executive in a fortune 500 company, the big house with the pool that served as a connection spot, the five-star vacations to Bermuda, Hawaii, or Aruba. And one of the most important things I had was confidence, or at least I had the appearance of confidence. I was a master at creating the illusion of thick skin. I had a leader once ask me, "Do you chew nails for breakfast?" He thought I came across too tough. I wasn't tough, though. I believed there was something wrong with me, that I needed to be fixed. I didn't think anyone else felt the things I felt.

I never let people know what was truly going on inside. Nobody ever knew the tidal wave of uncertainty that rolled around my insides like a hurricane. Nobody knew I didn't trust myself. Nobody knew the depths of my inner hatred toward myself, or the way I spoke to myself; so self-critical and judgemental. Nobody ever knew that I felt vulnerable, scared, and alone most of my life. I spent decades of my life feeling unlovable, unimportant, and not worthy of all I had or all I desired. I would be so mean to myself. *Who was I to want love? I was not lovable. Who was I to want to feel important to someone?* I never thought I was the most important person to anyone. I navigated my life very much alone. That is not a complaint, it is a fact. And I always looked confident, but I questioned myself over and over again.

Life didn't start that way. I was a loved daughter and youngest of three. I had a lot of friends growing up. I played softball, danced, played the flute, and generally was allowed to try anything I really wanted. All the little disappointments in life, all the teasing, all the little comments, were creating stories in my head. Research states that our brain takes in everything like a sponge from the time we are in utero to about eight or nine years of age. Our brains aren't developed enough to understand each thing as it is, so we make up stories and narratives with each comment or experience. They become the basis of a belief system that drives our behavior, action, or inaction. All of the stories I made up convinced me that I was never good enough; I was unwanted and not lovable.

I remember specifically having some of these "not good enough" feelings come up as a teenager. Different situations convinced me that I was not enough for anyone, especially boys. I remember being fourteen when a boy I really liked had to move out of our town. I knew we would never have the relationship I wanted, and I internalized that as a rejection. I was feeling very low and stood in my parents bathroom with a bottle of aspirin in my hand wondering how many I had to take to die. I thought that I didn't want to live if he was no longer around, and that I was not worthy to be around for anyone else. That was the first time I ever thought suicide was possibly an answer. It wasn't. I put the bottle away and moved on.

Depression, low self-esteem, and often self-loathing became a way of existing for me. I internalized and personalized so much around me.

I could feel so good about what was happening, and then one thing could be said to me and my mood would change instantly. This was the cycle I lived in for a very long time. Most people, unless they were very close to me and emotionally safe, had no idea how I really saw myself. I didn't like myself. I didn't think I was worthy of love, affection, and a family. I very often used anger to mask any other emotion. Anger was my go-to emotion. I had no idea it was masking intensely deep sadness.

I was thirty-two years old when my first marriage ended, and I was completely distraught. I had been in that relationship for sixteen years. I had no idea how I would navigate life alone. I remember when we split up, my brother called me to see if I wanted to move closer to him; at this point we were about twenty minutes apart. His words were kind and have stuck with me to this day: "I don't like you living all the way down there alone, I think you should move by us." I felt really loved and supported at that moment. My parents offered to fix up part of their house so I could move to them, but I stayed in my condominium because a new chapter of being a single woman was beginning.

It was after my first divorce that I went to therapy for the first time. I decided to join a group therapy program with other people who had gone through divorce. There were a few benefits for me in a group environment. The first was that I didn't have to talk or divulge if I didn't want to. Saying a lot would have forced me to be honest, and I wasn't prepared for that yet. Second, I got to see firsthand that others' situations were worse than mine. Many had been in domestic violence situations.

I didn't last long in group therapy because I thought I didn't need it. I was moving along, meeting new people, starting a new job, and feeling good about life. A few years later, I was on the phone with a friend who was also still friends with my ex-husband. She revealed to me, somewhat by accident, that he was getting married again. That call plunged me into depths of depression I hadn't experienced yet. While we were fighting at the end of our marriage, he continually said he did *not* want to be married. This call made me realize that wasn't fully true. The truth was he didn't want to be married to me. That hit differently. For days, I could not shake it. I had trouble working, sleeping, eating, and really living.

I have written about my feelings for most of my life. My mom was a great writer, she would write poems for birthdays and anniversaries. She would also write down how she felt, either in a letter that may or may not be mailed or shared, or on individual pieces of paper, many of which I found when I cleaned out her bedside table after her death. From her, I learned that writing things helped to process what I was feeling and to get out the emotions I couldn't seem to tell anyone else about. I had a diary as a child that grew into journaling as an adult. My journals really began toward the end of my first marriage, when I had so much to understand and get out. Much of my journaling then seemed to place blame and not look at me per se. One evening in the middle of my second divorce, I pulled out some of my old journals and found this entry:

May 1997

So he is getting married again. After he told me he didn't want to be married. Now I get it, he just didn't want to be married to me. I am unlovable, he was right. I am wandering through this life not knowing who I really am. I cannot seem to rise above the feeling like I am under water in the dark and cannot find the surface. There is no air. I am drowning.

Fast forward a few years after that phone call that informed me he was remarrying, I was remarried too, and life looked pretty great on paper, but the thoughts were louder than ever. I was feeling every bit of the pain combined with my shame. My second husband was starting to sound like the first one, and once again I believed I wasn't lovable. I wasn't good enough, again. Once I lost my uncle and my cousin, and watched them both be cared for so well by their children, I felt such envy. The realization that my decisions meant I had nobody to care for me, that I was alone in the world, ruminated in my mind. I believed that God punished me for my decisions. I believed the world punished me. I was angry at myself. I was angry that I let myself gain so much weight again as I ate instead of feeling, and I was angry that the weight made me undesirable to my husband as his touch changed. He made sure I knew that was about me. I was angry that I punished myself over and over again for decisions I made decades ago, and I was angry that, once again, a relationship with a man triggered my self-loathing.

That anger followed me everywhere, sometimes as self-deprecating humor, sometimes as true self-loathing. It hovered under the surface and at times came out swinging like I was ready for a ten-round fight with a heavyweight champ! With all of this going on under the surface, I still was going about my day-to-day routine with a smile when I could muster one. I would get up at 4:30AM, commute over an hour to work, work a ten-hour day, and then commute over an hour back home. My days were hectic, filled with meetings and constant pressure from my bosses. Even on vacation, I was expected to answer emails, be on conference calls if necessary, and be available if anyone needed me. Since my oldest brother's death I visited with my parents once per week. Even when I was married, I tried to do that as much as possible. But that meant I was also trying to keep my marriage from the predicted implosion. The days went on like this for a while. Constantly being busy, trying to hold it all together. Always thinking I was one step from being fired, or yelled at, or divorced. I was just waiting for the other shoe to drop constantly, and walking on egg shells because of it.

One day in late 2009, these thoughts were rampant as I was driving home from work. My husband was attending a zoning board meeting that evening and my brain was on overload. *How could this marriage be imploding? Why does he not love me anymore? What is wrong with me? I will have nobody to care for me if I need it when I'm old. I made the decision not to have children and now I'm going to lose my partner, too.* I could feel my heart racing as I drove. There was thought after thought and all of them were negative. *How can I stop these runaway thoughts? How can I stop the pain I feel? How do I stop the loneliness?* At that moment, there were tears in my eyes and I was focused on all the pain I felt. My brand new Jaguar with the 380-horsepower engine was careening down the country, windy road as my mind wandered. The car accelerated to sixty miles per hour and all I could think was, *I want the pain to stop.* Seventy miles per hour, *I don't want to feel this shame any longer.* Eighty-five miles per hour, *the world would be better off without me.* Then I saw it. This big, beautiful oak tree at the ninety-degree bend in the road. All I could think of was that I needed to hit that tree and be free of this pain. *The shame and pain would be gone. The world, my family, everyone would be better off.* As my car quickly headed for that tree, in a flash I saw my mom's face yelling that she could not afford to lose another child. I hit the brakes and the car spun a full three-hundred-and-sixty degrees, narrowly missing the tree and kicking up tons of gravel, the windshield cracking. When the car stopped, I sat there with tears streaming down my face, and realized at that moment that I did need help. I could no longer deal with this shame and anger by myself. Who was I kidding? I wasn't dealing with it at all.

I called my husband and let him know what had just happened before I drove home. I was sitting on my couch in my bedroom watching television when I heard the garage door open. It was only 8PM, he wasn't supposed to be home for another two hours. I ran downstairs into the kitchen and he held me immediately. I began to cry.

"What made you come home?" I asked.

"You. I wanted to be sure you were okay," he responded. All I could think to myself was, *Wow, maybe he really does love me. Maybe things can be okay after all.*

They weren't. The arguing became constant, and he would get angry at every little thing I said. I would try to make him laugh and he would take offense. On the evening before my thirty-fifth high school reunion, we had an event at a local bar in the town I grew up in. He came with me. As we were sitting there, a woman walked in that he knew. I had seen her once or twice and knew she was from the law firm he worked at. He had this little silly grin on his face and said, "Look honey, David's secretary is here." I thought it was strange and could see his mannerisms with her. They were different from how he was with other people. There was something I couldn't put my finger on, a chemistry I did not expect. They kept going outside the bar to smoke and talk while I was with my friends. It left me uneasy and that night I asked him about it. Of course he denied anything and let me know that this is just me being jealous. I believed him.

Two months later, his dad passed away. He and his father had a very complicated relationship. His father lived in California, so we had seen him only a handful of times over the five years we were married. We decided to fly out for the service. I always prided myself on being open with him, unlike the secrets I kept from my first husband. So he had full access to my phone and I had access to his, as well as each other's

Facebook profiles. The woman from work had sent him a little signal via Facebook, I saw it and thought it was suggestive. His reaction was over the top and unhappy that I would even think that about them. He was angry at me for everything. Early in our relationship, he appreciated my strength, problem solving skills, and speaking up for him. Now if I did, he was angry and felt emasculated. I was confused. He finally broke down about his dad in his step-sister's arms, never in mine. He told me I was not comforting.

By New Year's Eve of 2009, we were in a very low place. He was telling me he wasn't sure we would work out. I was begging him to try with me, go to counseling, anything to stay. We decided at 5AM on New Year's Day that we would continue to try to make it work. It was short lived. He only stuck around a few weeks. He had a lifestyle I created, and he wanted to keep that as long as he could. Although I saw what I saw with the woman from work, I believed that I could convince him to stay and that he was truthful when he denied there was anything between them except bitching about work.

January 17, 2010 is one day that I will never forget. The New York Jets were in the playoffs that evening. We had the entire day planned. We loved hanging out, eating, drinking, and watching sports. We were both very happy when we were present, in the moment. That was when our relationship was at its best. He drank a lot of Jack Daniels that day and after the game was over, I went upstairs to get ready for bed. I washed my face, brushed my teeth, and my hair. I turned to walk out of the bathroom and he still wasn't upstairs in our bedroom. I called down to him, no answer. I walked downstairs and he was standing by the kitchen sink crying. Cautiously, I walked over to him to see what had happened. He looked at me as he cried.

"I can't do this. I don't want to do to you what your first husband did, but I can't do this anymore." I was shocked. I stood there in disbelief not sure what to do. My survival instincts kicked in and I began to cry and beg.

"It's so late, you drank so much, let's go to bed and see how you feel tomorrow." Of course I swore we could fix this, I was committed. He walked upstairs, grabbed an overnight bag, and began to pack a few things. I have no recollection of what I said, or yelled, or cried at him. He walked out the door. I called his cell phone multiple times, he never answered or let me know if he was okay. I began to write a letter, telling him all that I felt, and again begging. I was trying to control what was happening, and it was all out of my control at that moment. I never slept that evening. On Monday morning, my friend called me to see if I wanted to go shopping. It was a holiday and we were both off from work. I just began to cry saying no, that my husband had walked out. She was at my house in ten minutes, holding me. It was an awful day.

He moved back in a few days later, mostly for economics sake, although I thought he really wanted our marriage to work. We went away for a weekend to our shorehouse, and again being in the moment allowed for me to believe we could work this out. He told me while we were there that he was going to rent something where his sons lived, and I wasn't going to go up there any longer. He told me that his sons really didn't like me and that they didn't want to come down to New Jersey to visit any longer. He was now going to rent a trailer in upstate New York and go see them there without me. I couldn't believe it. I had a good relationship with his sons, or so I thought. Of course I questioned that immediately, never trusting myself. He must know better.

In April, the "other" woman quit her job at the law firm to move to New York to work. My husband only said New York, he never told me that she was moving to the town his sons lived in and she had gotten a job up there. That was discovered by the private investigator I hired as I knew there was more going on. I also knew I needed to know one way or the other. I have always been the one to say, "Don't ask if you don't want to know the answer. If you do ask, be ready for anything." My PI set out on a Friday evening trailing my husband up the Garden State Parkway onto the New York Thruway. By the time I went to bed that night I knew he had met a blonde at a bar that she worked at and the two cars were driven to a small residence a few miles away. There were pictures of the cars, license plates, and the two of them on the porch smoking by the time I woke up.

That next day I was leading a group of employees at a community service event in Newark. My niece, Stephanie, was joining me. I was on the phone a lot of the morning, with the private investigator, with my brother, trying to figure out what I was going to do. I thought I was hiding my anger, sadness, and disappointment from everyone. My niece could hear some of my phone conversations.

"I know something is going on. Are you ok?"

"Yes," I said, as my phone rang in the car. It was his ex-wife, and the mother of his children.

"Suzy, he said he was coming up here this weekend, we haven't heard from him yet. He doesn't seem to be answering his phone either. Do you know where he is?"

"I do. Try 1313 Armstrong Drive," I responded.

"What are you talking about?"

"That is where he is with his girlfriend, I just found that out." There was silence on the phone. At this point, Chris and I didn't have much of a relationship because he had made sure of that. He definitely tried to pit us against each other during our marriage. I could feel the heaviness, she wasn't sure what to say.

"I'm good Chris," I said, filling the silence, "I need to go. I will talk to you soon." Years later, she told me she hung up and felt so bad for me. She and her husband had actually thought about talking to me before the wedding to tell me things about him I didn't know. I told her I wouldn't have listened. I had to learn this one myself. Fast forward a lot of years, Chris and I are good friends and really love each other. We both love her sons that she shares with my ex-husband, and because of that mutual love we are family.

My niece and I headed home. We stopped at my parents so I could tell them what was happening. My mom just looked at me and said, "I thought something was wrong." I stayed stoic and didn't cry. I was a strong woman who was going to move forward like the lion she was. Once again I was not chosen. Once again I was not good enough, worthy enough, or lovable. When I finally had confirmation that he was seeing a secretary in his office, I decided I was not going to let him get the best of me. By that Sunday, the locks on our house were changed, the codes to get into the garage were changed, and I had packed a lot of his clothes into the back of my friends' car.

He called me Sunday evening to say that he was going to stay one more evening, drive to work in the morning, and would be home Monday night. I told him not to bother coming home, his key did not fit in the lock any longer. He immediately got defensive.

"What do you mean? What are you talking about?"

"I know all about Michelle. I know you are there with her." He told me I was crazy, knowing that was one of my big triggers. I yelled at him, gave him the address he was at, and told him I had pictures if he wanted to see them. He was silent. I told him I would be at his office at 9am and hung up the phone. I felt the strongest I had in a while.

Early on Monday morning, my friend and I drove the thirty minutes to his office. He came outside trying to gaslight me, telling me that I didn't know what I was talking about, that he wasn't seeing anyone and he didn't understand what pictures I could have. I placed his stuff in the back of his car, let him know he was a man with zero integrity, slapped his face, and walked away. I felt strong, I felt invincible. That feeling lasted all of twenty-four hours. The next day I felt empty. I was scared. I was again embarrassed as the woman who could not keep a man. I started to believe all of the horrible things he had said to me; that I was hard to live with, and unlucky in love.

I knew after my suicidal thoughts that I did need some additional help and support. Although I was always a journaler and that helped me through so much of my life, I needed much more now. I didn't believe in God, or anything bigger than me. I lacked faith in myself as well. Therapy this time was different. I told her the truth, unlike my last two therapists. I told her about my abortion. I told her about my ruminating thoughts. I told her I felt completely unlovable. I was honest with my therapist and myself for the first time in my life. At forty-eight years old, I finally recognized that I had not been truthful with myself for too long. I never regretted the decision I made to have the abortion, but I did regret that I never did anything to help myself afterward; I buried it.

What I have learned since then is that you have to feel your feelings in order to heal them, you actually have to acknowledge what and how you are feeling. Shoving your emotions down with food, drugs, being constantly busy or on call for your work twenty-four-seven, will not help you in the long run. The emotions are stuck in your body and will cause you physical ailments as much as emotional. I have learned you have to acknowledge them and release them in order to heal what has hurt you. Once you get honest with yourself and feel what you need to feel, you actually begin to trust yourself more. Once you get honest, you realize you have been running from something, not toward anything. Running from that voice that was deep inside, the inner voice that was trying to get my attention and let me know that I was suppressing too much, was ignored for far too long. I heard it all the time and ignored it. Learning to really trust your intuition and inner wisdom in a world that ignores it is difficult. Do it anyway.

So, you may be wondering where all of this lack of self-worth and trust was coming from. That answer requires going back to the beginning...

CHAPTER 2

I never thought I was really wanted. I am the youngest of three, and the only girl. My brothers were eight and five when I was born. Given the years of difference and my mom's age, I was always told I was an "oopsie baby." An accident. Not planned. The one they didn't expect. My mom, after a particularly difficult argument we had, wrote to me. In her letter she reiterated that my birth was the best day ever. She prayed for her little girl and I finally showed up. It took me over 30 years to realize that I was not an 'accident'.

Prior to my birth, the family spent the summers at the Jersey Shore. They would rent a house in Belmar, and my dad and uncle would go each weekend, and for their annual two-week vacation. My brothers viewed this as some of the best fun they ever had. Our parents had bought a house in Woodbridge the summer after I was born; "the country" was what my dad called it. My dad and my uncle no longer felt they needed to get away from the city for the summer. Once I was born, summer at the beach no longer occurred. I was teased often by my older brothers that life was better before I was born. Their child minds thought my birth was the catalyst to no longer going to the beach for the summer and, as many big brothers do, teasing me was their specialty. They teased about everything. My red hair that made me different, my birth ending their summers at the beach, my deep emotions and quickness to cry...it all made me an easy target for them, and they were at times relentless. Some of that teasing lasted well into my thirties.

Growing up in the 1960s and 1970s was fun personified. As kids, we were outside most of the time. The street I grew up on had twenty houses on it, and were brand new when we moved there. Almost every house had children. Ages ranged from ten years older than me, to about five years younger. There was always someone to play with. The kids on the street would play hide-and-seek, red rover and other classic games all summer long. My brothers and some of the older boys would often play stickball in the street, which was always fun to watch. We would block the street on the 4th of July and have a great block party that filled our street and even extended to an adjacent park. There were water balloon fights and egg tosses and three-legged races. During the winter, we couldn't wait for snow storms. Our street had a big hill that went downward toward the cul-de-sac. It was the best sleigh riding around. The innocence and freedom of my childhood is something I will always cherish.

At the age of five, my mom went to register me for kindergarten and found that my name was incorrect on my birth certificate. She wasn't going to let that slide and trekked to Jersey City to have a new certificate issued. My original certificate said my name was Susan Joy Domenick, my new one issued in 1966 had my correct legal name, Suzy Joy Domenick. Again, something to tease me about. My brothers used that as a way to try to convince me I was adopted. The red hair that nobody else had, the two birth certificates, and the years between us created a relentless wave of teasing their little sister. And my brain took it all in.

One of the best parts of my childhood was living three houses away from my aunt, uncle, and cousins. My cousin Valerie was like my older sister. My cousin Jack was another brother. My aunt and uncle were my safe place when I didn't feel safe in my house. Whenever I would get angry at my mom, I would "run away" to my aunt. We would talk and then I would go back home. We were five kids raised by four adults. Our vacations together were great! Whether it be Niagara Falls or Florida, going on trips together was always fun. We were the original Griswolds, having adventures on each vacation. One year, we hadn't left our town yet and were at the drug store picking up whatever prescriptions my parents needed. Mom came out to the car and told us to not say a word, Dad had cut up the wrong credit card and now we had to go to the bank. As soon as my dad got in the car, the three of us couldn't hold in the laughter. At first dad was a bit angry and then we all had a good laugh that we couldn't even get out of Fords! For me, one of the most difficult parts of growing up was not having a sister. My cousin was nineteen years older than me, and moved to Florida by the time I was seven. I had other female cousins who I was close to, they weren't day-in-day-out sisters, though. I really didn't have that feminine energy to bond with. I always thought that if I had a sister, then we could fight back against the teasing. Maybe if I had a sister, she would help me really see me, the way my aunt helped my mom see herself.

When I went to elementary school the teasing continued from my classmates. I will never forget when my mom cut my hair in second grade. Yes, most moms did cut their kids' hair then, and my mom was no different with me. She cut my hair into the shortest pixie cut ever. When I went to school, the kids in class started laughing and asking who the new boy was in class. I laughed along with them, always trying to please whoever teased me. When I got home, I broke into a flood of tears, yelling that she was never going to cut my hair again. And she didn't. My hair grew past my waist, and I did not cut it again until eighth grade. The embarrassment, the teasing, and the beginning of body image issues all created a young child who was always looking for approval and acceptance. I was always looking to please people so they wouldn't make fun of me, they would like me or maybe even love me. My self-deprecating humor began then. I would make fun of myself before someone else could. It felt powerful to beat them to the punchline . Really, this humor just added to my comparison, self-judgment and critical inner talk. The effect of these disappointments was a lot of shame, guilt, and a feeling of unlovability.

My parents would tell me to ignore my brothers' teasing. They were only kidding and I needed to learn to take the jokes, they would say. I was told that I needed thicker skin, and that I was too sensitive. Those words have haunted me my entire life. I remember even having a teacher in high school talk about my tears. He chuckled and told me to toughen up a little. I took all of these comments in and made them mean something about me. My belief was that I had to fight to be seen and heard, I had to fight to be here. I wasn't allowed to be soft, feminine, or girly. I remember even being made fun of because I threw a softball "like a girl." None of these things on their own were big issues or traumas, however, in my little girl brain that wasn't developed yet, all of it meant that I wasn't loved, accepted, or wanted the way I was.

I had to fight to be seen. I had to fight to ensure people loved me. I needed to please people, do what they wanted to be loved. In school, I never believed people wanted to really be my friend for me, I always thought they wanted something. I had to fight for space so I became loud, funny, and self-deprecating. I became a people-pleaser so that I could feel loved. I would laugh at jokes that really weren't funny and often mean-spirited, especially laughing hard when that sarcasm was at my expense. I completely internalized any type of teasing and made it mean I wasn't good enough, worthy of love and did not belong, at all. I was different from the rest of the family, far more intuitive, far more in touch with my emotions, and I believed that made me less than. I was called too emotional, thin-skinned, cry-baby, and crazy all too often. All words that conjure up a lot of negative feelings for me even now.

I was raised by feminists. My mom, the child of Polish and Jewish immigrants, wanted to be an independent business woman. She wanted to go to college, not be married. In the 1940s that just wasn't expected of women. Although she attended college for a year or two, she then met and married my dad. Her focus was to always ensure that I was so independent, and that I didn't need anyone. As a child, it seemed to me that my mom treated the three of us very differently. I think all kids think that and I think most parents do. I didn't like it because I always felt she was tougher on me than them. Steve, the oldest, was the responsible one and she counted on him for a lot. Jeff, the middle son, was the comic and he entertained my mom a lot. I was her baby and only girl who she had big hopes for, and always treated me that way. At times she pushed me harder than my brothers because she wanted an independent girl. She knew how the world was changing and she wanted me completely prepared for that change. She was raised by a very independent and strong woman and wanted me to be the same.

My mom's parents emigrated to the US in 1919 with their baby son in tow. My grandfather left on a boat first, three months before my grandmother. He was in steerage and the ship he was on went a circuitous route to New York City. My grandmother left after him with her mother and baby. Both ships landed in Ellis Island on the same day. My grandfather spoke fluent German, as did my grandmother, and he was able to find a job quickly with a German man who owned a hardware store. A few years later, my grandparents purchased that store and ran it until the late 1930s or early 1940s. Their son passed away at the age of two from scarlet fever. My mom was born just after that. I have always wondered what impact having her brother die right before she was born had on my mom. I always wondered if that was the beginning of some of her insecurities.

My dad was also the son of immigrants from Italy. His parents came to the United States earlier than my mom's, also with their first-born son. Dad was the youngest of four children. By the time he came along, his siblings could translate for him and he never actually learned a lot of Italian. His parents showed him what hard work would do for him. In both my parents' eyes, work ethic was something that you had to display. That was something nobody could take from you. Dad quit high school and joined the Navy at seventeen-years old to fight in World War II. He talked about his time in the war and defending the world against fascism all of my life. He was an extremely proud veteran.

My dad was also a feminist. He had no qualms with my mom keeping her maiden name as her middle name. She didn't like the idea of what she viewed as giving up her identity and my dad agreed. He was always tougher on my brothers than on me. I had him wrapped around my pinky the moment I was born. Dad was loving and soft with me. I rarely was yelled at by him as a child, different from the expectations he had for my two brothers. He, too, wanted me to be independent, although he didn't go about it with the gusto Mom did. At five years old, my dad had me under the car with him so he could show me what an oil pan looked like and how you could take off the wingnut to drain the oil out of a car. He wanted to be sure I understood cars so that no mechanic could take advantage of me. He had me lifting little weights with him as he wanted me to be strong and wanted me to feel that power.

Throughout most of my life, I had a close relationship with my mom. When I was hospitalized at five, she stayed on a cot next to my bed for the duration of the stay. She taught me how to ride my bicycle even though she did not know how to ride. She was tough on me in terms of grades and school, she was loving when it came to what I wanted to do. I wanted to be a brownie and a Girl Scout, she said yes. I wanted to start dancing ballet and I did that for seven years. Mom had a lot of style and would buy very cool clothes for me. In 1971, at ten years of age and before women could actually have a bank account in their own name, my mom bought a blank checkbook from a stationary store. She looked at me with such a big smile, "I want to teach you how to manage your money so you never need anyone else." Her view was that I needed to become the independent woman that she felt she was not. Each month we would sit down and she would give me fake companies to write out checks to, and we would balance the checkbook. She didn't do this with my brothers. She knew the world would have expectations of me as a woman and she wanted me prepared. There was never a doubt in her mind that I wasn't going to be successful. She projected her need for independence and success onto me. I have always shared this story as a way to help people realize that my independence was drummed into me from the time I was quite young. I give my mom big kudos for thinking about what was happening in the country and in the world.

Women were on the precipice of being able to have bank accounts and credit cards without a man cosigning. She wanted to be sure she set me up to have the life she had once hoped she would have. As much as my mom loved my dad, she always felt she was born a little too early. Had she been born later, she may have been able to finish college and have a big career. That was what she wanted for me as well. She got it, as I created a successful corporate career after getting my degree. What also came out of all the ideas and comments about independence was someone who was hyper-independent. I never would ask for help, or take it if it was offered. I felt as if I didn't really need anyone, and, unfortunately, my husbands both felt that way as well.

Mom projected so much onto me, not because she wanted to hurt me, but because she was so unhealed. My mom had a lot of anger inside of her. We all do when we have unrealized trauma. She knew that rage was inside of her, even if she wasn't sure why. Mom was always on a diet when I was a kid. Her body to her was ugly, fat, and undesirable. I had no idea what positive body image was, I only ever heard negative things about her. When I sported a curvier body once I was a teenager, she immediately got me a bikini. She liked how I looked. My beliefs around my body and what was accepted in society and what I "should" look like were emblazoned into my psyche at a very young age.

There were times in my childhood that my mom seemed to be afflicted by weird and unnamed illnesses. When I was about ten, an uncle that my mom was very close to passed away. My mom was distraught as this uncle was like a dad to her after her dad passed away. Uncle Leo was my grandmother's youngest brother and he was not married. He spent a lot of time with my grandmother and with us. He would come stay at my aunt's house and visit with us often. Right after he passed away, Mom lost her voice. She could not talk above a whisper. She went to ear, nose, and throat specialists, they couldn't find anything wrong with her vocal cords. Her voice was so soft that we had to strain to hear her. She would clap loudly if she wanted you to come to her, even our dog knew her clap. Dad, Mom, and I drove up to Boston for my mom to be seen by doctors at Lahey Clinic. The day mom had all her tests, Dad took me to Salem, Massachusetts so I could see the houses and places where the witch trials occurred. I was fascinated by that entire time in our country and couldn't understand why women were murdered for being witches. The doctors at Lahey Clinic were as stumped as every other doctor, they couldn't find something actually wrong.

A few years later, another uncle passed away. This was my dad's sister's husband. Dad was very close to him when they were younger. They lived in the same town as us and as soon as his sister called, my parents ran to the house to be with her. Not long after that trauma, my mom's voice miraculously returned. No explanation from any doctor. Of course a few said it was psychosomatic, which then always seemed to mean there was something wrong mentally with the person. What I know now is that my mom suppressed a lot of emotions and they took root in her body. Her inability to really be honest about how she felt probably led to her losing and gaining her voice through trauma. She also had optic nerve paralysis at another point in her life, again probably more emotional than physical.

Mom compared herself to her sister often, thinking she wasn't as smart or pretty as her sister. I learned the art of comparison in these moments. I compared myself to other women often in my life...perhaps I still do at times. Mom's desire for me to be better than her was her driving force to push me. If I came home from school with a ninety percent on a test, she never said great job. Her first comment was always, "Why didn't you get a one-hundred?" All of that was internalized, I took it all in to validate that I wasn't good enough and I wasn't worthy unless I was perfect. The beginning of my perfectionist journey is completely intertwined with my core beliefs of never being enough.

When my first marriage fell apart, Mom and I hit a very rough patch in our relationship. Mom's comments would activate my feelings of inadequacy and I would then take it out on her. She pushed many of the same buttons my ex-husband pushed and then some. She was quick to tell me that if I did not lose weight I would never meet another man.

Nobody would ever love me as a chubby girl. Once again I believed I was unlovable.

Mom had quite the temper. She would blow up quickly and many times not even realize what she said out of anger. I was the same way. I remember many years later, my dad was staying with me as he recuperated from a number of weeks in the hospital. He and I had a bit of an argument and I really yelled, which was not something I did very often with him.

"You are a lot more like your mother than I ever thought, he said.

"That didn't sound like a compliment," I said, laughing nervously. His face did not change, there was no smile and he answered me.

"You know I loved your mother more than life, but your mother had some things...and you have those same things." I knew immediately he was talking about my temper and the words that fly out of my mouth in anger.

"Yes, I do know that. I don't know why there is so much anger, but it's there." He finally smiled before answering me.

"It would be good if you could figure it out and have less of it." *It would be good,* I thought. It didn't happen overnight. I did have to look at why there was so much anger. What I found over the years was that my anger came from immense sadness. That sadness was rooted in so much. I believe some of it was generational and some of it came from the belief that I was never really wanted.

My mom was Jewish, and when she and my Italian-Catholic father married he was excommunicated from the Catholic church. He refused then to raise us in the church, which my mom didn't want either. They decided not to raise us in any religion and instead taught us about both religions to let us each decide. We had a Children's Bible that mom would read to us at times. I was allowed to go to Saturday mass with my

Catholic friends and Friday night Sabbath services with my Jewish friends. I was encouraged to read about other religions. Although, I now can look back and say that the freedom from indoctrination allowed me to be free of all the fear that religions seem to enhance, it also left me void of real faith. I had no faith in anything bigger, not a God, not the Universe, not Angels, nothing. I believed all we had was us, and we had to make everything work for us. I didn't have any religious trauma, however I lacked faith. Our beliefs as a family really focused on working hard. Work ethic was strong and was the thing that was going to make you successful. You only needed to have faith in yourself.

My parents were both first generation Americans with immigrant parents and were children through the Great Depression. My dad's family was very poor, he was taught at a young age that success was brought by working hard. That focus on work was so strong that we were taught that unless you were so sick you couldn't get out of bed, you should go to work. If we had a fever, we went to work or school as long as it was not over one-hundred degrees. Work as hard as you can, that is how you are rewarded. We all were what I would call "workaholics." As depression babies, my parents possessed a scarcity mindset, and believed that hard work would keep you getting what you deserved. You couldn't risk losing your job. You didn't take risks that may not work out, as you needed to keep the job at all costs. I learned at a young age that you kept your head down and just worked. If you did a good job you would be recognized and rewarded. We all worked at young ages. Making money was a priority in my family. I was a babysitter at the age of thirteen and also a softball umpire. I worked from that time on.

A scarcity mindset took hold of me differently than it may have in others. I learned early to save my money. My mom's mantra was, "Make a dollar, save a dime." I definitely did that. I also didn't want to live always worried and always lacking what I truly wanted. I watched my mom not buy furniture, or skip having the house painted when it needed it, because they didn't want to spend their saved money. I didn't want to live that way, and once I made a lot of money I didn't. I decided to spend my money more than my parents did. I used credit cards for the things I couldn't afford. That set me up for a lifetime of racking up credit card debt and then wiping it out when I received my bonuses. At times, I would buy just for the sake of buying. I would always buy the better brand, stay at a nice hotel, and spend. I loved having the money to create a lifestyle that included luxury vacations and an ability to go out a lot. At the end of my second marriage, he told me that one of the hardest things for him was to leave the lifestyle I had given him. It wasn't about the life we had, it was about what I could give him and do for him.

As I got older, I became the person that would do whatever anyone else wanted to do because I believed if I didn't they would no longer want me around. This didn't show up as people-pleasing to others. It always just looked as if I was agreeable, until I wasn't. I remember one time, just after college graduation, when I committed to help my friend move and set up her new apartment. I had to renege as my dad wanted me to stay home and help him get the house ready for my college graduation party. I had to break that commitment which created issues for us for a while. She was hurt and angry that I couldn't help after I committed. I had over-committed and didn't navigate it well. I was afraid to let anyone down. Of course when you approach life thinking that everyone is one issue away from leaving you, your fear creates built-up resentment. That resentment would be released as anger, with big responses to small disappointments and an inner feeling of no trust in myself.

I decided to attend college at the State University which was twenty minutes away from home. The deal I struck with my parents was that I wanted to live on campus, unlike my brothers who both commuted. They agreed and one of my close friends from high school and I decided to room together. Living away at college gave me such freedom. I was not under anyone's supervision. I could do whatever I wanted. That first semester was an opportunity to just let loose, and I did. I partied heavily and reunited, unbeknownst to my parents, with my high school boyfriend who they made me break up with. I had nobody to answer to about going to class or doing homework or grades. I decided half way through the semester that I no longer would attend my calculus class. I would read the book and ask my roommate questions. I didn't like the professor, and again I could skip if I wanted. That didn't work out well for me, I failed the course. My dad, being a mechanical engineer, had taken every calculus class ever. I was so ashamed that I failed, I couldn't tell him over winter break. I waited until I went back to school to tell them I failed, via the phone. My dad's disappointment came through the phone. I had let him down. I had let myself down. My pre-med major would change, I knew I was not cut out for all the sciences and calculus classes ahead. I decided to take a psychology course to make up for the credits and fell in love.

I changed my major to psychology and entered a program in school that would lead to an internship in human resources. This was the 1980s, internships were not the norm. I loved the coursework after that and really dove head first into psychology. The best part about college was my roommates. We lived together in an apartment for three years. Different women, different personalities, and a lot of fun. We did a lot together. We shopped, cooked, and ate meals together almost each night. We looked out for each other at parties and generally went out together much of the time.

Moving to college and becoming an adult did not lessen my feelings of inadequacy. I think it may have intensified them, honestly. Now I had to prove myself to my roommates, my professors, my parents, and, because I was so insecure, I needed to prove something to myself, too. I continued to be filled with disappointment, shame, and guilt. As I reflect on that time, I can again see my people-pleasing tendencies, my ability to take everything personally, and my shame. And I hid things from the women who I thought were my best friends. I judged myself so harshly, that I chose not to tell them everything.

There was a guy who we all knew. His name was John. He and I became really good friends during our sophomore year. By the end of that year, we both thought there might be something more between us. We were going home for the summer and promised to continue to talk to each other and see how we felt. We each had a significant other. We would talk on the phone almost daily that summer, very often late at night. I had my own phone in my room so I would hide it under a pillow at night keeping my parents from finding me talking into the wee hours of the morning. By the end of the summer, we agreed that we couldn't wait to get back to school to see each other and that we thought it was time to split with our current partners so we could date.

I excitedly got back to school, so looking forward to seeing him. We were moving into our apartment when our friend Patty came over to tell us about a terrible motorcycle accident that happened the day before in South Jersey. John was killed. I stood there in disbelief. Everyone was shocked. We were all quiet. I couldn't let them see how this impacted me. I believed they would judge me for having feelings for someone when I had a boyfriend, even if nothing more than talking late on the phone happened between us. So, I held it together and said I needed to run out. I got in my car and burst into tears. *How could that happen? How could he be dead, we talked two days ago?* I didn't know what to do. I started to drive around the campus aimlessly, crying and screaming. My heart was heavy and breaking. *Why didn't he wear a helmet?* It wasn't the law yet, the helmet law came after his accident.

It was one of the most traumatic experiences of my entire college experience and nobody I lived with could know I was such a mess. The day of the funeral, I proceeded to get very drunk. I snuck into the chapel on campus to sit in the back for his service. My friend Chris spotted me and came back to get me. He moved me up front to sit near him and his girlfriend Donna. It was the only time someone held me with compassion and sympathy regarding that loss as nobody else knew what we meant to each other; not even Chris knew about us, he thought I was mourning only as a friend, not a woman falling in love. I carried that pain alone from that day forward.

I now recognize that my inability to tell my best friends things because I was afraid I would lose them showed up a lot. I also always worried about what others thought of me. Their opinion was more important than my own. I remember one year when we came back to school after winter break. I used to get salon size shampoo and conditioner bottles from my friend whose family owned a beauty supply store. I loved the brand and loved that I didn't have to buy it often or at retail. I put them in the bathroom and walked into my bedroom. All of a sudden, I heard one of the women say, "Oh look, the big bottles are back!" And then the group laughed. *Wait, they talked about this without me?* I immediately took that as they were unhappy with me, and internalized it completely. I felt embarrassed and hurt. I didn't say anything though, in fact I think I laughed along with them. If

I admitted it hurt my feelings, it would make them dislike me, or so I thought. So, I kept it to myself and held a little grudge for a long time. I had a lot of those grudges built up and I know that build up came out at different times through anger. I look back at that Suzy as I write this book and realize how she took everything as a criticism and a judgment. If this happened today, I would genuinely join in on the joke, not feeling less than, but feeling accepted.

My levels of comparison also became clearer in college for me. I compared myself to everyone. I compared my grades, my lovelife, and my body to others. I looked at everything as good or bad, right or wrong. I started to have sex with people at school. Looking back, this was the start of thinking I needed sex to feel loved. At the time, I thought I was a normal college student having fun after parties or going to the bars. This tendency to need external validation and acceptance didn't end when I joined the work force after graduation. I didn't completely trust myself and I always wanted to be the fixer or the hero. That got attention and a pat on the back, which I needed so desperately. I would volunteer to take on work or projects that may not have been mine. I also was willing to actually take responsibility to fix things that others may not have done well or right. I would jump in and do other leaders' jobs at times. As one boss said to me, "Suzy, I love that you fall on your sword, but I wish you wouldn't fall on other people's swords." That hit hard. I got it, I always took responsibility for what I or my team did or did not do, and very often took responsibility off of other executives. I used to think I did that just to be collaborative, believing it's what made me a good partner or coworker. We win together and we lose together, right? After years of reflection, I now know I also did that to be the hero and to please people.

Our little child minds take in so much information that we give meaning to things that aren't real. I learned to be hard on myself, and it lasted most of my life. How could I ever feel good about myself if I was constantly critiquing myself? The disappointments, the shame, and the guilt did not end once I grew up and went to college. They actually became stronger. My deep feelings of shame and self-doubt were validated over and over again. Once I believed, to the core of my being, that I was undeserving of the things I really wanted, and that I was so different from everyone around me that I was unloveable, my life choices were impacted. The way I carried myself was performative and it was exhausting, but I didn't dare question how I was raised or what I believed; I moved through life the way I was expected to, and hoped that somewhere along the way I would start to feel better.

CHAPTER 3

I went to the bathroom and spotted some blood in my urine. *That's strange*, I thought, *why would I be spotting? That's unusual...*I was at Busch Gardens in Tampa and had just come off the rollercoaster. I was twenty years old and heading into my senior year of college. I walked away from the bathroom with an uneasy feeling that I kept to myself. I had just learned that my niece, who was born two weeks prior, definitely had Down's Syndrome. My sadness for my brother, and fear of not knowing what all of it would mean for my niece's quality of life were weighing heavy on my heart. That sadness turned to shame about two weeks later.

At that point I had been with my partner for four-and-a-half years when we found out I was pregnant. He was my first real love and the first person I had ever had sex with. We met when I was about fourteen or fifteen and he was a year older. We met through mutual friends, and we all started to hang out from time to time. I was reeling after the boy I thought I loved moved away. At the same time, his best friend was moving away. We commiserated about those losses, both of us afraid that we would lose our best friends completely.

He was very funny. He was always able to make me laugh. He would ride his bike the five or so blocks to my house and we would talk outside for a bit about our losses and our summer. I would babysit at a house around the corner from him and sometimes he would stop by and we would sit outside and talk. He loved sports as I did and we found we could talk for hours very easily. I remember at one point his best friend asked me if I had any desire to have sexual relations with someone from Fords. I looked at him confused and asked what he was talking about. He finally told me that he was interested in going out with me. I remember feeling so excited that someone I was interested in was interested in me, too. I said yes and he came over that following Friday evening. We walked in the park at the end of my street, my dog in tow, and at the end of the night he kissed me to seal the deal. We were together off and on throughout high school, and he was actually with me that day at Busch Gardens when I saw the blood in my underwear.

My first thought when I saw the blood was that I could never tell my mother or father if I was pregnant. I never wanted to see the look of disappointment on their faces that I saw when this happened with my brother and his girlfriend five years prior. All I could think was I did exactly what my brother did after I swore I wouldn't. I heard my parents' conversations about his situation. They wanted to send me away to Florida to live with my cousin Valerie so I wasn't present for any of it. I heard my mother discuss abortion. I also heard my grandmother tell her that no matter what this was her grandchild and she needed to love and accept the baby. I had no idea that my parents' disappointment was more about the girl who my brother was with and not about their own child. All I knew was that I was never going to give them a reason to have that look of disappointment on their faces if I could help it. But then I got pregnant before graduating from college, and I made a lot of assumptions from a place of fear and guilt about what that meant.

We made the decision and the arrangements quickly. We were going to Planned Parenthood in Woodbridge. It was a beautiful, unusually warm day in September. With only each other and our thoughts, he drove me to the stark grey building on Route 9. We both were silent on the drive there. Inside, my mind was racing. *What if I knew someone when we got there? What if someone saw his car as we drove there? What if I didn't wake up from the anesthesia and became braindead? What if I died?*

As I got out of the car, I saw the people standing outside with their signs. There was red paint that looked like blood on one of the signs that read, "BABY KILLER!!! YOU WILL ROT IN HELL!" Another sign was plain black and white and said, "ADOPTION OVER ABORTION!" I walked by them, he was ushering me into the building so no one would hurt me, as fear and shame flooded my body. It was like a scene out of a movie or something; I was shocked and horrified.

The facility was so sterile and cold, not a place to help anyone feel better or even safe. I was asked multiple times, by multiple staff members, if I was sure that I wanted to make this decision. I never wavered from my decision. After I stripped down and went into the surgical room, I cried. I hoped that I would be okay and that I would never have to think about this again. I had never been so scared in my life, and I felt so alone. Of course, I knew my boyfriend was scared as well and there for me, however, in the end this was about me. He never wavered from agreeing that this was my decision, and I knew he would support me, whatever I decided to do. I was so grateful when the procedure ended and I opened my eyes. The prospect of him having to tell my parents I died during an abortion was so frightening to me. I was worried about dying, sure, but I was more worried about what my parents would go through if I died in that manner; always worrying about others before myself.

After the procedure we drove to Roosevelt Park so I could rest a bit. The park is a big beautiful one in Edison. It has a lake as well as many groves for picnics and a theatre. It was a beautiful day and we both brought school work with us to try to keep our minds occupied. I couldn't think beyond what I had just done. I remember sitting with him, wondering what this meant for our relationship. *Would our relationship survive this? Will he still love me? Who should I tell? Is this mine to bear alone?* Both of us wondered out loud if we could make it through this. We saw friends have abortions and then break up, and we weren't sure if we could survive. What I never anticipated was that this would be the wound that would follow me for life. I thought, given my conviction that it was the right decision, that I could move on easily. It wasn't easy. I did everything to ignore it. I did not tell many people right away. In fact only one of my four roommates was told, even though I was close with all of my roommates. All of the secrecy was difficult, and I started numbing my feelings with food and alcohol. Whenever anyone asked me how I was doing, I was quick to say, "I'm fine," even if it felt like I was drowning under the weight of it all.

The roommate I did tell never made me feel judged, but the shame just sat in the pit of my stomach. I could barely look at my brother or sister-in-law at times. I loved my niece, it was never about her. It was the guilt of depriving my brother of a healthy baby, as if my pregnancy could have been theirs. I went home less that semester, because I was afraid that somehow my mom would figure things out. I also started to party even harder, attempting to stop the shame but failing miserably. That shame stuck with me for a long, long time.

The Monday after the abortion was my twenty-first birthday. I spent that day drinking my feelings. I washed down all the shame, guilt, anger, self-doubt, self-pity with any and all of the alcohol I could stomach. That was easier than feeling. I shoved my feelings down about many things moving forward. That became a coping mechanism for me, and

I started to live by the mantra, "Work hard, play harder!" I lived by that mantra for decades as a way to keep the mask from slipping away, and to avoid revealing to the world that I was an unhappy mess.

He and I married when I was twenty-four years old, and I truly believed we could make it as a couple. We both had gotten through the trauma and still believed we never wanted children. As our marriage grew, so did my inability to really love myself. It reignited the feelings I had as a child, that the world was better without me. Life was better before I entered it. That shame, guilt, and blame was too heavy. I tried to convince myself that my self-hatred was normal. *What woman really loves herself, anyway?* I tried to convince myself that I healed that wound of shame, and that my self-hatred was just normal stuff brought on by not fitting society's definition of beautiful. I seemed confident on the outside, but I was a frightened child on the inside. I would lash out to try to control things. I often felt out of control. I had no idea I really had no faith in myself, or in anything bigger than myself, nor did I truly trust myself, my intuition, my decision making.

I once described my relationship with my first husband as passionately in love and passionately in hate. We were not good at communicating and both of us seemed to hold a lot inside. We had quite a history and it was definitely baggage. We would often hurl hurtful words at each other during arguments, dragging up old wounds. We had a lot of fun together, but we also made mean-spirited jabs at one another, pretending they were funny and not hurtful. I was taught to laugh off teasing or hurtful comments from my brothers, and carried this into my relationship with men. Our fights could get explosive, though. In the middle of one of our fights, he was so angry he threw a wine glass at the wall. It didn't break, it just stuck in the wall. We both began to laugh which ended the fight. I wanted to put a frame around it, but he refused. He was embarrassed he lost his temper like that. We both did that often though, even in high school. He would get into a lot of fist fights when we were in high school, and people were definitely afraid of him. He was big, worked out a lot, and had a temper, although most people never saw it. I wonder now if that temper showed up in our relationship more as a reaction to my own actions. About seven years into our marriage, I suggested that we consider having children. Most of our friends had started families and I was beginning to feel as if I wanted that as well. He did not want children. What I didn't know then was that he was already starting to feel as if the marriage was not going to last. He didn't see children in our future because he didn't see me in his future. He didn't explain any of that though, so once again I believed I wasn't loveable enough to have what I wanted.

During the last two years of our marriage, I lost a significant amount of weight. I had gone to my doctor and she felt I was too heavy given I was on birth control pills. She thought that there was a risk of stroke if I did not lose weight. I had been on diets most of my adult life, many of them fad diets that never worked in the long term. I worked to lose twenty-five pounds and I loved how I felt and looked. I walked differently, and I moved in the world differently. I wanted and enjoyed the comments and looks I received from men. I felt sexy and, at the time, being seen as sexy meant being seen as worthy to me. Receiving a lot of validation from men meant I was worthy of their affection and attention. That attention led to my affair. I didn't love the man I had the affair with, and looking back I'm not sure I even liked him, but he made me feel loved and desirable. I liked how he made me feel. I knew I wouldn't stay with him and I believed I wanted my marriage to last, but my husband didn't make me feel the way my lover did. I felt sexy and beautiful with him, something I hadn't felt in a long time.

The man I had the affair with was one of my colleagues at work. I was a Personnel Manager for Macy's and worked at our Newark building. I managed store personnel as well as support administrators in accounts payable, accounts receivable, customer service, and other smaller roles. When I was promoted into the position, my boss let me know that I was the youngest person he ever promoted into what was considered a Senior Executive role. Working in retail always meant that the hours were not typical. I worked weekends and nights often. I was also commuting about forty-five minutes or so each way to work. My work days were long and my job was stressful. One day I was standing in this man's office, trying to solve a problem that involved both of our departments, when he just looked at me and said, "You are so beautiful. I have never been so drawn to someone." Before I could respond, he kissed me. I was stunned and walked out of his office without saying a word. We ended up talking about it a few days later and next thing I knew I was in an affair at work.

My marriage continued but my husband began to pull away a bit. I remember going on a vacation to the Bahamas as a way to try to save our marriage. As we walked down the hall together, a very good looking woman looked at him and said, "Hey baby, you are hot! I'm around if you want some of this." I stood there dumbfounded. *Did she not see me there?* He did nothing but smile. He didn't put an arm around me, he didn't tell her to fuck off...he just smiled. When I got angry, he told me to go to hell. At least that woman admired him, he said, and I didn't. It was at that moment that I realized his body had also changed and I hadn't paid attention to that. He had cut out carbs for six weeks and his muscular frame was cut like a bodybuilder. *How did I not even notice that? Was I so involved in my affair and my job that I didn't pay attention to my husband?* I realized at that moment that I wanted to fight for my marriage. I did not want a new partner as much as I wanted the attention. I made the decision to end my affair after that trip and focus on my marriage. By then though, he had already checked out, and looking back, I could not blame him. We tried marriage counseling. That was a bust. He said whatever he thought I wanted to hear when we were in with the therapist and then would tell me it was all a lie when we got home. He would say he loved me and wanted the marriage to work, just to get through the hour. I, of course, thought he meant it so when he really wanted out of the marriage, I was dumbstruck.

At the time of the separation and divorce, I most certainly did blame him. I justified our divorce to myself for a long time, telling myself that the affair was not the reason for the divorce because he never found out about it, so the fault was on him. But this was a futile attempt at coping with everything I contributed to the unraveling of our relationship. He was far from the perfect husband, especially when his temper took over. I was constantly self-deprecating, lashed out often. I never seemed to realize that we both had to walk on egg shells around each other. He started to pull away from our marriage long before my affair started, but that didn't justify my affair.

One evening as we were struggling with whether we were going to stay together through the Christmas holidays or separate beforehand, we went to dinner with a group of friends. We bickered throughout the dinner. Everything I said, he would nitpick, and vice versa. We made the entire table uncomfortable until it became an all out fight. We walked out of the restaurant and were fighting in the parking lot. Our friends were trying to get us into our car and he would not budge. He stood in the middle of a road, refusing to get in the car and go home. He screamed at me, "You are completely unlovable! Nobody will ever love you!" He walked away and didn't come home that night. Those words would not have hurt me so badly had I believed in myself and loved myself more than I did, but I had no faith in myself. I didn't trust or love myself. I believed I was undeserving of love, so his leaving the relationship made a lot of sense to me. I believed that God was punishing me for my abortion, even though I didn't have much faith in God or in anything when my first marriage fell apart.

Years later I told a friend that I believed I was being punished, and her response left me dumbfounded. "My God doesn't judge or punish, he loves." *If God wasn't punishing me, then why was I free falling toward rock bottom?* My marriage imploding was very difficult for me to deal with and process. I was angry. I was sad. I was humiliated. I was embarrassed. And most of all, I felt as if I was a victim. I remained very angry for a long time. And that anger created a chasm between me and a few of my friends. I could not believe that a few of my friends from college were trying to remain friends with my soon-to-be ex-husband. A couple of years after we split up, I remember feeling very uncomfortable at a get together. People were talking about my ex because they had just seen him. I realized that I was having too much trouble being friends with them since they were remaining friends with him. I was angry and couldn't wait to leave. I stopped talking to those friends for a very long time, and resented them for making that choice.

My anger and my inability to be mature at the time of my divorce drove me to lose friendships. I tried to convince myself that I didn't need people who still wanted to be friends with him. I tried to convince myself that they were wrong and I was right. As I have healed and grown I realize that I am completely responsible for the change in the relationship with my friends. I realize just how childish my reactions were. Now I can look back and realize that I was so driven by the belief that I was unlovable that I was self-sabotaging. I am not proud of it and have worked to forgive myself. I have also done what I can to reconcile with that group of friends. It will never be what it once was and I will never be a part of the group the way I once was. I own that. As I heal and become a version of myself that accepts and loves all of me, being honest about past behavior is transformative instead of just painful. Learning to forgive myself took many years and many different twists and turns.

One of the practices that has helped me fully forgive myself and others is the Hawaiian Ho'oponopono prayer. It is a beautiful practice for reconciliation and forgiveness and centers around a mantra: *I'm Sorry. Please forgive me. Thank you. I love you*

While in meditation or sitting quietly in a chair, you can repeat these words over and over. This practice helps to acknowledge responsibility and take ownership of actions. The mantra calls for seeking forgiveness from self or others, expressing gratitude for the opportunity to heal and grow, and emphasizing the importance of self-love and connection. This practice can help promote self-compassion and create inner peace. It took me far too long to realize that I was judging and punishing myself, believing that I wasn't good enough to have the things I desired. I was the one who believed I wouldn't be a good mother. I was the one who made it true that all of my fuck ups and insecurities would be passed down to a child. I was the one holding myself back from true happiness because I wasn't questioning the narratives I had been conditioned to believe about myself or what my life could look like.

In coaching we have what are called "little t" and "big T" traumas. "Little t" traumas are the ones that cause emotional distress, but did not occur during a life-changing event; they're more common traumas. "Big T" trauma stems from catastrophic, life-altering events that change every aspect of how you're living and how you view life. I didn't know anything about "little T" and "big T" trauma when I was going through my divorce, but I wish I had. I left that marriage truly believing all of the things my big and little traumas were making me believe, and those beliefs informed my decisions for the following decade.

CHAPTER 4

For the next ten years I looked for love and acceptance from others without fully loving or accepting myself. I looked for these things with anyone who was a willing partner. I didn't really understand what love was, and looked for it in every face I met, every bar I went to, and every man who gave me the smallest bit of attention.

My love story ended in 1993 after almost sixteen years together; we grew up together thinking that we would grow old together too, but it wasn't meant to be. His rejection rekindled my feelings of unworthiness, and when I found out three years later that he was getting remarried, my feelings of unworthiness intensified. I buried myself in work because I was important there; people needed my leadership skills and I could communicate at work in ways I only dreamed of in my intimate relationships. At work I was seen and heard, but in my personal life I felt completely invisible.

When we divorced, I began a new role at a bank on Long Island, a role that catapulted me in my career. I was working alongside a financial services executive who believed that he needed two roles to stand in lockstep with him, finance and human resources. He viewed us as his right and left arms. I remember telling him that I wanted to learn more about the financials of the bank and especially how the branches made money. He had never had a human resources executive want to understand that and he was very excited. He immediately called the territory chief financial officer into the office and asked him to spend some time with me. Tom, the Vice President for the territory, was a brilliant businessman. He was a good leader who could get things done. He helped me really improve my skills and I soaked up the opportunity and attention. I worked alongside some excellent human resources professionals who helped me to become better and better. Once I became the Vice President of Human Resources for a territory, I helped the organization recruit, develop, and manage a workforce that crossed sixty-six branches throughout Long Island. Many days I would drive out to my office in West Hempstead in Nassau county and then have to drive further east to meet someone or visit a branch.

Commuting to Long Island meant two hours each way every day. I left my home at 6am and returned at 8PM, sometimes later. I thought it was perfect since, in my mind, I had no life. Most of my friends were married, many with children, so I had very few opportunities to go out. I do know now that I never would have had the stellar career I had if I had stayed with my first husband. I would not have taken the role in Long Island which really did help me improve and become a better human resources executive. He never would have liked me driving two hours each way, and knowing how I was at that time in my life, I would have turned down the opportunity to appease him. There was a lot of wear and tear on the car and on me, plus I doubt I would have wanted a job at the company he worked at if we stayed married; working and living together would have been too much for the both of us. Yet, twenty-one years of my thirty-five-year career were spent at the same company he worked at, and there were even a few years when I was the head of human resources of a business he was employed at.

Even though I buried my nose in work most of the time, I managed to meet and create a friend group. Unlike so many of my married friends, this group was younger and single, so we socialized a lot. "Work hard, play harder" was now not only my personal motto, but the motto many of my friends lived by, too. A big piece of "play harder" for me was sex. I craved it. I craved it with whatever man was a willing partner. Sometimes it happened in the front or back seat of a car, sometimes at a hotel, and sometimes I was stupid enough to bring a stranger back to my home. I put myself in many dangerous situations. I didn't care. Perhaps I had a death wish then and didn't know it. Perhaps it was all that shame and guilt, although at the time I thought I was just a strong, independent woman getting what she wanted and needed. I was also really good at reeling a guy in, and it gave me a boost in confidence every time, but the boost never lasted very long.

I never really thought about the danger of it all until one evening. I was partying at a hotel bar and met this very good looking guy. After a number of drinks I found myself in his hotel room, on the bed. As I opened my eyes I realized I was naked and didn't remember taking off my clothes. He was naked and coming toward me, and in that moment of clarity I realized I didn't want any part of it. I jumped up and grabbed my clothes. I hastily got dressed and left. I was scared. I knew I hadn't had enough to drink that I would almost black out and be undressed by someone. I realized I might have been drugged. I jumped on the elevator, pressed a button and away I went. The elevator doors opened onto the banquet floor, fortunately after an event had concluded. The servers were breaking down the tables as I started to walk through the ballroom. A young girl ran over to me and took me back toward the elevator. She fixed my shirt that was disheveled and not buttoned, and made sure I was pulled together. She asked me if I was okay and put me on the elevator to the lobby. Once there, my friend who was frantically trying to find me screamed, and rushed me to a cab. The reality of it was that I could have been raped or killed. That moment was my wake up call to not be so bold and cavalier about my safety. It still hadn't dawned on me that my behavior was being driven by shame or lack of self-love.

The friend group I created introduced me to Jack. Jack was a heavy metal guitarist who was loud and funny and for some reason that I still cannot explain, he was sexy in my eyes. I have always loved music, especially rock and roll. I wasn't always in love with real heavy music like he played, but I became a fan to stay close to him. He and I became friends quickly. I would stop at his house on my way home from work and talk to his parents, even visiting his mom in the hospital more than once. Jack had a girlfriend, however, I knew I was falling for him and I wanted so badly for him to want and need me. I was being a people pleaser and trying to control the situation without realizing it, and my pattern of falling for people who were not interested or not available began.

About a year after I met Jack, the band he was in put out a new CD. One of the songs was called, "She Fell in Love." As I listened to it, I felt like it was written for me. The chorus had a line that stuck with me. "She fell in love, with no one to fall on." I fell for Jack and he wasn't there for me to fall on. I felt as if this had become an unavoidable part of my life. I was in love with my first husband for such a long time, and now he was marrying someone else. Every guy I met either had someone else, or slept with me before deciding I wasn't good enough. Nobody loved me, or so I believed. I always tried to act as if that wasn't real and that I didn't want any of these men. I lied. I lied to myself the most. I acted like all of this sex was just me being a woman in her thirties and early forties. I acted like everyone would do this if they weren't married. Although I thought I was bed hopping out of desire, it was really out of actual need. I needed to be hugged. I needed to be kissed. I needed to feel something. I had spent a lot of my life trying to not feel because I was always told I was too emotional.

My career took off during this decade, and once I felt I had the job security, I proudly sold the condo that I originally owned with my first husband and bought my very first free-standing house. I also had the opportunity to live and work in Japan for six months during one of my human resources assignments. That experience allowed me to grow so much. People thought I was so confident and strong going off to another land where the language is so different to work on an acquisition, which was a really big deal. I kept wondering if, at some point, people would figure out I didn't know what I was doing, even though I was very well trained and very successful. I remember focusing on all of the wrong things as I prepared to leave, even to the point where I assumed I wouldn't like the food there, and maybe I would lose some weight. I wasn't thinking about the positives at all, choosing instead to focus on my fear and the negatives that came with that fear. The self-doubt followed me all the way to Japan.

It was a fourteen-hour flight, and I had never flown quite that far. I left at 9AM on a Saturday and arrived at Narita Airport outside of Tokyo at noon on Sunday. It felt so strange to me to lose a day like that! As I got out of the airport, I looked for the bus that I was told to take. There I was with two huge suitcases, a briefcase, and a large purse trying to get on a crowded bus. Fortunately for me, the bus driver spoke English and ensured I was on the right bus. It took us over two hours to get to my hotel. I was exhausted, scared, hungry and a bit excited. I did wonder if I could do the job. My self-doubt was screaming at me that I had no idea what I was doing, and that I didn't belong, but I persisted.

The following day, I sat in a large office with four other people who all worked together in New Jersey in the International businesses. I was an outsider. There was one woman who was about twelve years younger than me, and three men who were a little older than me. The first thing I had to get used to was sharing an office, desks, the three phones in the room that were used for dial-up service for our computers, and the back and forth conversations in both Japanese and English. It was sensory overload at first. The streets were crowded, the trains were crowded. Everyone was hustling around me all the time, and I felt like I was barely keeping up.

It felt really hard to build relationships with the employees of the company we were acquiring. Of course, they had a lot of pride working at this firm that was now in bankruptcy and they had no idea what our company was really going to do. The individuals who were there from the United States seemed intimidating to the Japanese. We spoke to each other quickly, using acronyms and company speak very often. The people who were there from the international group knew each other very well and had some inside jokes and certainly a rapport that I couldn't compete with at first. I started noticing that as a woman I wasn't taken as seriously by some of the Japanese men and that just continued to erode my confidence. This was 2001, and women were seen by most in Japan as second class citizens. Western women, like me, were a little higher on the totem pole than a Japanese woman, but nobody was ever as important as the men. I remember going out to dinner one night by myself. I walked into a sushi place that I went to with someone I was working with only days before. I often dined alone at home, but as I walked in alone, every person stopped what they were doing and looked at me. I felt like I was under a microscope. I was the only woman coming to dine alone. The other women were either sitting with a man or were serving the food. It didn't matter what language was being spoken, I could tell I was sticking out like a sore thumb. I sat down at the sushi bar and the man next to me started talking to the chef in Japanese. He looked at me a few times during the conversation and it became obvious it was something about me.

"American?" The chef had shifted his attention to me.

"Yes," I responded.

"From where?" he asked with a heavy accent.

"New Jersey," I said.

"Ah! Jersey, what do you want?" He smiled and looked at the man next to me and said something that seemed to stop him from bothering me. That chef helped me get through that evening. I remember going back to my room and just crying my eyes out. This was not going the way I had hoped. The leaders didn't seem to want to work with me, and the head of the business wasn't sure how to work closely with human resources people like me. I felt very out of place. By the end of the second week I wanted to go home. I called my mom and started crying. I told her I thought the company made a mistake, I wasn't the right person for this role. Mom's words still stay with me today as she said, "Your company asked you to do a job that it believes you are capable of. You stay there and show them they were right."

Again, I was questioning my abilities, questioning myself. This is a pattern that I didn't really notice until then. I knew what to do, I just didn't know how to get it done there. Instead of realizing that, I internalized the difficulty relating with the Human Resources department as something wrong with me and my leadership style. Was I too direct? Was I not helpful? Mom pushed me to realize that even if I was not sure I could do what was being asked, the company was. This was my opportunity to prove that to myself, just like I was giving my nephew the opportunity to prove himself.

I spent some time with the younger woman who was also there, Jenna. Jenna was brilliant, a Harvard graduate, and we connected really well. I shared with her how I was feeling and we talked through a lot of my feelings. The next day she shared that she let the head of the business know that she thought I was really good and smart and that he should spend more time with me. They had a relationship already, and I was the new kid. After that day, things began to click. I focused my approach to be less directive and more curious. I asked more questions and really helped connect dots for people. The human resources department assigned an employee, Ando-san, to me who spoke English to be my liaison with the department. He could get me information, help me with who I needed to talk to, and help explain things to the head of human resources if he didn't understand what I needed. Ando-san was a lovely, spiritual man who really touched my heart. He was smart, well-read, loved hearing about the United States, and was filled with compassion, and a willingness to learn. He had a great sense of humor as well. We spent a lot of time together. I told him I was named after a 1940s actress named Suzy Parker. The next day he came into the office with a book he had at home about American actors and actresses. It was the first time I had ever seen a picture of her. She was beautiful. He made a copy of that picture for me, and I still have it to this day.

About two weeks into being there, a group of information technology analysts came to work with us. I knew them from the last international project I was on, as well as my work as an HR business partner. I finally had a few friends there. We all began to go out a few nights a week, eating together and trying new parts of Tokyo. One Friday evening, a group of us went out to a club in Roppongi where there were many US marines on a weekend leave from Okinawa. Standing at one of the bars, I started talking to an absolutely gorgeous young man. He was only twenty-four years old and his face was truly perfect. In a matter of minutes we were kissing. My friend came over to say he was getting us a taxi and this young man and I walked out to it together. Thomas came back to my hotel with us and left a few hours later. Sex was a way for me to feel loved, and even in Japan I needed to fill that void. He wasn't the only person I had sex with in Japan. I also met an Italian man who was there learning how to drive the bullet train, a high speed train that was also coming to Italy. I was in a brand new place, but still stuck in my usual patterns.

The first time I came home was about six weeks after I left. I was so excited to be home. My dad picked me up at the airport and Mom had the dinner I asked for ready; pasta e fagioli, bagels, egg salad, and tuna salad; foods that were next to impossible to find in Japan. I tried to acclimate back into my life for a week, but it proved very difficult. Over the six weeks I was gone, life had moved forward for everyone without me. My life felt like it didn't move forward, just moved differently. I would share stories and be surprised by the lack of real interest. Everyone was caught up in their own lives, and I wasn't a real part of and of it for six weeks. I felt disconnected from everything and everyone around me, and began to long to go back to Tokyo.

Once I got back to Japan, I decided to spend a weekend exploring by myself. I took the train to the old city of Kyoto. Steeped in Buddhism and history, it was completely different from Tokyo. As I walked the famed Path of Philosophy, lined with beautiful cherry blossom trees in bloom, I remember thinking that I was doing what I never believed I could do. I was seven-thousand miles away from everyone and everything I knew and I was making friends, making an impact, and growing. I was more capable than I had given myself credit for. My confidence as a leader started to grow. My insecurities seemed less intense. I decided to visit a Japanese bath house while I was in Kyoto. This was a beautiful Ryokan, a traditional Japanese Inn, with beautiful baths, both inside and out, with mineral waters that were so good for you. Most of the women walked around the bath house naked. There was no outward appearance of shame. In fact, they walked around as if they had never felt shame around their bodies. I stood there wondering if I was going to be naked or wear the bathing suit I had brought. I decided that I actually would look more strange with the bathing suit on, so I stripped down and started my way to one of the baths.

It was a beautiful place with nooks and crannies where I could easily sit in an area alone. I could go outside and let the sun warm my face as I was in the bath. I did both. I found areas to just sit and think, and I found areas where I could float around a bit in the sun. Most of the women spoke only Japanese, but the smiles were enough to know I was accepted. During my time going from bath to bath, inside and outside, my focus on my flab, my cellulite, and my body disappeared. I started to just float and enjoy how the water felt on my skin, instead of assuming people were staring and judging. It was the most freeing feeling to let go of my disdain for my body. Being there with these women who had no body image issues allowed me to release my judgement for a while. These body image issues have never completely disappeared, I have had them forever, but this experience was unexpected and has stuck with me to this day.

Our company's plans to acquire the company from the bankruptcy trustee worked as well as possible, and by the end of the six months I had helped achieve the acquisition. For my part of the project, we offered over one-thousand people targeted retirement plans and had over seven-hundred people comply. We exceeded the number we needed, and did it in a way where people left with dignity, money, and strategies to invest that money. The company was acquired in May of 2001, and we all received very handsome bonuses. I received so much more, though.

As I was preparing to leave, I held a dinner with the HR department. I gave them each a New York Yankees hat, and they gave me a Yoriyumi Giants hat. We had gone to see that baseball game when Hideki Matsui was in town. I wanted to share my favorite team with them. Ando-san handed me a separate gift after everyone left the dinner. It was a handmade coffee mug that he had made himself. As we sat quietly, he turned to look at me, and with tears in both of our eyes, we said our goodbyes.

"I've changed because of you," I said, letting the tears fall down my cheeks.

"And I have changed because of you," he nodded before continuing, "I have only love for you." We hugged and that was the last time I ever saw him. He helped me to better understand spirituality. I still wasn't fully in my spiritual awakening journey, but he was the person who talked about the Buddhist temple he would go to, and shared the peace he found in meditation.

I walked away from Japan learning more than I ever thought possible. I was able to create new relationships with deep connections in six short months, and I managed to do that completely outside of my comfort zone, seven-thousand miles from everything and everyone I knew. I adjusted my leadership style and approach, which I brought home with me and which helped me take my career even further. I had evolved. I still occasionally used sex to fill my voids and feel loved, but I didn't use food quite as much. I started to embrace my body differently, learning from the Japanese women that our bodies are ours to love and honor. I began to open up to spirituality and understand Buddhism more.

CHAPTER 4

I met my second husband a few years after I returned from Japan, about ten years after my first divorce was finalized. One of my best friends told me there was an attorney in one of her client offices who was just out of a relationship and was interested in dating. She thought he was really nice and asked if I would like to meet him. *Why not? I hadn't ever been set up by a friend, maybe this was a good thing.* We decided to set up a group meeting at a bar with karaoke, and we had a great time. We had some drinks, a few appetizers, and sang along with each person who performed. He decided to sing a solo. I remember watching him and thinking how wonderful it was that he was willing to put himself out there like that. I had only ever done karaoke with someone else. He sang "I Saw Her Standing There" by the Beatles. It felt as if he was singing that directly to me. He came back to us with thunderous applause and we all decided to go up together and sing "Paradise by the Dashboard Lights" by Meatloaf. It was such a fun evening. We talked, sang, danced, and kissed. It felt like a dream, it was so easy. I remember him telling me that night that his dad always said, "Burnham men don't dance." All I could think was how cool it was that he was dancing with me, not being constrained by the idea that he wasn't a good dancer. We shared phone numbers and left when the bar closed. He asked me to text him that I was home safely, and before I was even home he called. We spoke for the rest of my drive home. I got home, too excited to sleep. This man was intelligent, an attorney, good looking, and we just had the best first date I ever had. By the time I got to my desk the next morning, there was an email from him:

Dear Suzy,

It was so great to meet you last night, I had the best time. When you walked into the bar, there was a bright light around you. I have been glowing in it since. I look forward to seeing you again soon.

Wow, I thought, *I hadn't had someone write something that beautiful in a very long time.* I felt a smile come to my face and a flutter in my tummy. Maybe I was finally going to find my person, my partner, my soulmate. Two days later, we had our first solo date. He came to my house with a beautiful bouquet of flowers. We walked into town for dinner where we sat outside and talked for two hours. We talked about our childhoods, our jobs, our marriages, and our divorces. He told me a little bit about his sons. By the time dinner ended, I knew I wanted to keep getting to know him. I was already thinking that he was exactly what I wanted.

We didn't rush into sex, instead choosing to get to know each other first. When I told him I didn't want to rush into sex, he told me he was in no rush either. He had his sons to think about, anyway, and had moved to a different town to make it easier to see them more often. I really respected the way he parented his boys, and watching him be a great dad to them made me fall for him even faster. We spent eleven months getting to know each other before getting married. Our wedding was in the backyard of the brand new home we purchased together; our dream home. Each of his sons, now my step-sons, would have their own room, we had a gorgeous master suite, and the backyard was simply stunning.. The house was almost like a resort, and it felt like a reward for all of the hard work I had to do to get where I was professionally. I bought the house with my money, and the mortgage was only in my name. It was only when we went to purchase a home that I found out he was about two-hundred-thousand dollars in student loan debt, and that he hadn't been making his loan payments. He did offer to sign a prenuptial agreement so that I would know he wasn't just marrying me for money, and I did think it was a sweet gesture, but I planned on this marriage lasting forever. I thought he was completely perfect for me, or as close to perfect as I could get. Unfortunately for the both of us, his trauma had not been healed and I thought mine was fully healed but it wasn't. Our emotional baggage from separate, unhealed traumas caused so many problems in our marriage that I never could have seen coming. This was the relationship that brought me to my rock bottom, and catapulted me into my real healing journey, which led to me writing this book.

CHAPTER 5

I spent so much of my life thinking that I worked well under pressure and stress. I thrived in chaos, and I believed it was a superpower. Little did I know that was part of something that I had no idea was running my life; perfectionism. Perfectionism is a fear of failure disguised as high standards. Perfectionists, like myself, have such high standards that it is difficult to meet them, therefore if something doesn't come out perfect, we can blame the high standards and not ourselves. We didn't fail, we just have really high standards for ourselves. We sabotage ourselves with these false high standards, though, because they erode our confidence, they make us work harder not smarter; and they cause us to beat ourselves up.

As a child, my mom was the one with the ridiculously high standards. She had an expectation that I could be perfect all of the time. My mom's insecurities around her own intellect were the driving force behind her pushing me to be perfect. Although she never said those words, her questions and pressure made me believe that I had to be perfect to make her happy, and for her to love me. And so, a perfectionist was born.

What I have learned is that perfectionism is a fear of failure hidden in high standards. Reflecting on how that showed up over the years, I can see where those high standards got in the way. From trying to perfectly script a marriage to always trying to be perfect at work, my need to hide my fear of failure was evident. Others may not have seen it, but I would internalize each thing that didn't go well for me, and tell myself I didn't deserve the success I so desired. I could spiral down the rabbit hole of self-loathing so quickly if I made a mistake, even a small one. This mentality blew up any confidence I did have. I would wait to complete something, paralyzed by fear, and then complete it under the pressure to get it done. I always thought I was just great under pressure, never realizing that I very often created that pressure out of fear.

Perfectionism showed up in my relationships, too, especially my marriage. My second husband and I were complaining to each other that we had gained weight and we wanted to get back on track to health. We were married, after all, and vowed in sickness and in health, so after some resistance on his end, we decided to begin a health journey together. It was a Sunday in January 2010, and I asked if he would come with me to a track near us as I wanted to start jogging. Running was never something I loved, I would rather walk, but everyone I knew who ran as exercise was thin and I wanted to get thin. We pulled up to the track, and even though it was cold out, we started walking the track together to warm up.

"I'm going to run, but I doubt I can make it around the track," I said, expecting him to give me a half answer, but he didn't. He stopped walking and just stared at me. I paused as well, and before I could ask him what was going on, he spoke.

"You do that all the time!" He said, his tone filled with frustration.

"Do what?" I asked, genuinely confused.

"You decide you can't do something before you even try," he said before walking away. He was done with the conversation, and was going to finish his workout with or without me. I couldn't respond because I was stuck in my own thoughts. *I always come up with a reason why something isn't going to work out. He's right...whether it's a new recipe or even a workout, I assume it will go wrong before I even start. I do it at work sometimes, too...I spend too much time ensuring something is as close to perfect as it can be, even though perfect doesn't exist. I have a habit of setting myself up for failure...he's right.* The thoughts consumed me as I tried to finish working out. *Why do I never feel validated? Why do I feel like I am so undeserving?*

My fear of failure contributed to my lack of confidence and erosion of self-worth. My fear of failure combined with the beliefs I firmly held that I was unlovable and unworthy of love, left me unable to love myself; I had no idea how to love myself. I masked a lot by performing and using humor as a mechanism of distraction and defense. I would stand confidently on a stage and deliver information. I would stand confidently in meetings, sharing strong opinions. I was a contrarian very often and never realized that some of that was my trauma. I needed to be heard, to be seen, to be listened to. Having a different point of view would do that. I always followed my morals and values about what was right and wrong. My anger unfortunately came through at work as well, and eventually landed me in some hot water. It was a typical day at work when my boss called to talk to me about a complaint that was made about me.

"Suzy," he said, in a calm but serious voice, "I received some feedback that you were very angry last week and cursed on a few occasions. The word that was shared with me was 'fuck,' and I'm sure you know that we cannot tolerate that, or the hostile and toxic workplace it creates."

"Absolutely," I said, going into performance mode as my mind raced. "I take full responsibility, it will not happen again." We ended the call on better terms, but I wasn't worried about my own anger or how to improve my anger management skills, I was most concerned with who had made the complaint in the first place. I had a great relationship with everyone on my team, and I couldn't believe that someone would complain about me. I was livid. I was getting ready to take a week off of work to go on vacation and promised myself I would drop it; I wouldn't let it happen again.

I walked into work the next day, my last day before vacation, and walked into one of my team member's offices. I will never understand why I chose to talk with her, or why I didn't have any remorse. Instead, I started complaining to her that I couldn't be myself in the office because people were complaining about things I said that may not be "corporate." She just listened and didn't offer much. I left her office and continued to prepare for vacation.

While I was on vacation, my assistant called to tell me that my boss wanted to see me in his office in Jersey City on the following Monday. I was not to go into my office, but instead go directly to his office. I had never been called into his office like this and knew it wasn't going to be good. He had already warned me that my anger would not be tolerated, and I had let my anger follow me to work. I used it there to express disappointment. This was the worst aspect of my leadership, and I was horrified and embarrassed that I could lose my job. And I did. The following Monday he told me that I would be let go. I would receive a small severance package and I was to leave by that Friday. I never told anyone the truth. He and I worked through an exit statement that simply said he decided to flatten out the organization and my role was no longer needed. Although true, they were flattening the organization, I would have been kept had I not had these outbursts. He helped me save face, something I was very grateful for at the time, but sometimes I look back and wish he hadn't.

I sometimes wish I had to face the full impact of my behavior. I was spared the public embarrassment, and I was spared others' negative opinions, but I wasn't spared from myself; I beat myself up about what happened for weeks. I was out of work for a few weeks and then got my first of three consulting roles that helped me stay afloat for two years before I began working full time again. My traumas, my beliefs, and my stories caused my anger to flare up too easily, and that caused me to lose my job. I knew I needed to do something to help my anger, and group therapy was where I started. It was a start, but I was stuck in comparison mode when listening to others in the group share, and I was able to hide in group therapy. It was a start, but not a very intentional or effective one.

Fast forward a few years and I decided to go back to therapy, this time in private sessions, because I was feeling as if I was depressed. I lacked self-esteem and self-worth. Dr. Ellen was my doctor, and I felt as if all she wanted was to get me to retell the same, painful stories and cry about the same things each week. When I would tell her I felt like all I was doing was crying, she would just laugh, never really confirming if it was part of my care plan. With hindsight, I don't think she set out to just make me cry, I think she was a skilled therapist and knew I was holding an awful lot inside and not sharing it with anyone. I now understand that crying is the number one way the body releases trauma and expresses emotions so her seeing me cry was evidence that I was releasing and feeling my feelings, something she obviously knew I needed. I had no idea I wasn't actually feeling my feelings, or that I had so much I needed to let go of. In our weekly sessions, Dr. Ellen would help me reframe situations with my brothers or my mom, and helped me work through some anger issues, but I never told her about the abortion. I never told her about the shame. I never told her the depths of my self-loathing and self-judgement. I never told her that I thought if I died things would be better. I still wasn't completely honest; not with my therapist and certainly with myself. I figured I was fine and that what I was going through was normal.

As I started to become aware that I didn't really like some of my behaviors or actions, I started looking for ways to change. One day, I was watching *Oprah* and she was talking about this place she went to in Arizona that she said was, "like a spa and so much more where it's so easy to reset and recharge." She shared that this place, Miraval, helped her with some of her healing through her traumas and shame. *That's it,* I thought, *that's where I need to go.* I decided to book five days by myself at Miraval and was there in April of 2003. This amazing place focused on mind, body and soul, and helped me to begin to unravel the emotional knot that was buried deep within me. I first began meditation and yoga there, and began to learn about mindfulness, something I had never paid attention to before. I had never meditated before that trip, and it did not come easy to me. As an extrovert, sitting in silence for a prolonged period of time did not seem possible. The first meditation class validated this for me. I walked into the meditation room and met the teacher, Mary-Grace. I took a mat and sat down where I could lean against a wall, as I wasn't great at sitting cross-legged on the floor. Mary-Grace began guiding me and about twenty other people through the meditation. After about five minutes of listening to her soothing voice, I opened my eyes. I started looking around at the group and got consumed by my own thoughts. *I sat with her at dinner last night. What was her name? She was in yoga this morning, she was strong and flexible. I wish I was that strong and more flexible.* For the remainder of the meditation, I looked around the room and created stories about everything and everyone. When the meditation ended, I walked up to Mary-Grace.

"How do you get your brain to stop?" I asked as she gave me a small smile.

"Your brain has a job and it is to think. Meditation doesn't stop it, it slows it down. Try it again tomorrow without any expectations." And I did, every morning I was there. I loved the peace I felt afterward, and by the last day knew I wanted to try to do more of this. I purchased her guided meditation CD at the store and took it home to use.

One of the offerings Miraval has is to work with horses and therapists at a nearby horse ranch, their equine experience. I love horses, but never get too close after a bad experience at seventeen years old. I wanted to get over that fear so I joined the group at the stable. The first thing we did was take care of the horses, brushing them, cleaning them, and especially cleaning their hooves and shoes. Horses are so special, and they are known to reflect the energy of who is near them. They can read you better than you can read yourself. I was working on the horse, brushing him and petting him, and it was great. Then I went to pick up a foot to begin to clean the shoe and hoof. The horse would not lift his leg. I laughed before I tried again. The horse just looked at me and refused to lift his leg. I laughed more, trying to stay lighthearted and make a joke out of it, but tears threatened to break through the laughter. There was a therapist walking around who came over to me and asked me how I was doing. With a halfhearted laugh and tears streaming down my face, I said, "He won't lift his leg for me."

"Are you okay?" she asked, noticing the tears combined with laughter. I realized at that moment that I wasn't okay. I was embarrassed. I wanted to do it right, and not draw extra attention to myself. My energy was tight and stressed, which was not welcoming to the horse. The horse couldn't relax with me because I was too focused on all the wrong things. That revelation was eye-opening. Where else in my life did I try too hard to be the best, or to get the accolades because I didn't feel them as a child? Work. That was why I leaned into over-effort, and why embarrassment caused me to cry and run away. This horse reflected everything about my energy back to me. Once I dropped my guard and didn't worry about being the best, and once I no longer worried if the horse did what I wanted it to do, the horse lifted its leg for me. He even nuzzled me after his feet were clean. I was able to walk him around the field with his nose pushing into my neck every now and again to remind me he was right there with me. This experience stuck with me, and now whenever I begin to feel embarrassed, I remind myself of the horse mirroring my energy. I allow myself to feel that moment again, and then I very gently move forward without internal judgement. The shift at Miraval pivoted me toward my spiritual awakening, a process that led me to being a more open and honest version of myself, but I use the word process for a reason. The shift did not happen overnight - not even close - and when I returned home, my day-to-day routine really slowed down the progress I had started making at Miraval. The people I was around were not really focused on things like mindset work or spiritual connection, so it was easier for me to not focus on those things. Life went back to "normal" until catastrophe hit my family in October of 2003.

CHAPTER 6

My phone rang as I was waiting in the O'Hare Airport for my flight to Cedar Rapids, Iowa. It was my dad calling to tell me that my oldest brother, Steve, was in the hospital; they believed he had a stroke. He was awake and alert, but had paralysis and couldn't really talk. The prognosis at that time was good, they thought they stopped the bleeding in the brain, and I flew home two days later, just as he was placed in a medically induced coma so that his body wouldn't have to work so hard as they monitored the continued bleeding. Two days later he had no brain activity. He wasn't going to make it. My sister-in-law asked me to talk to my parents about organ donation; she couldn't do it.

As my family sat in the waiting room, I sat across from my mom and dad and shared that Betty and their four kids had talked and would like to donate Steve's organs. My mom looked at me with such pain in her eyes.

"Are you telling me my son is gone?"

"Yes, Mom," I choked on my tears. "There is no brain activity."

"You are my strongest child," she said, and my eyes met hers. She stared at me so intently as she said, "You have to get the family through this." My marching orders were received. So many moments after this I thought about how it should have been me who died. My brother, my parents' first born child, was so loved. He had a great marriage of twenty-seven years and all four of his children adored him. Too many people were suffering because of his death. *If it were me, that would be it,* I thought. Of course, I knew my parents would have been hurting no matter what, but there would be no spouse or kids anyone had to worry about if it were me who died. My siblings had their own families, I wasn't part of any family except my parents. *They would all get over it unscathed,* I told myself. I spent many nights wishing and praying it had been me and not him.

Before his passing, I had a few experiences where I felt my grandmother around me, but not many. I didn't truly trust my intuition or my gifts, so those moments were fleeting, until Simon and Garfunkel. Two months after my brother died, a few of my friends and I went to see Simon And Garfunkel at Madison Square Garden. It was one of the first tours they had done together in many years. Once we got into the city, I started to feel very anxious. I wasn't keen on the crowd and kept feeling somewhat claustrophobic, not something I had ever dealt with before. My brow started to sweat, my heart was pounding, and I felt as if I could crawl out of my own skin. I didn't want to be there with all of these people. I wasn't ready to have fun. I didn't want to laugh, sing, dance, or anything close to those things. Grief was taking over and I was plummeting. I sat down in my seat and never actually got up until the end of the show. I sat fairly rigid and remember I barely spoke to my friends. When the duo played Sounds of Silence, I felt the lump in my throat grow. The tears in my eyes began to slide down my cheeks as I sat there softly singing. All of a sudden, as I closed my eyes, I could feel arms reach around me and give me the biggest hug ever. There was no one there, and I knew at that moment it was my brother. Simon and Garfunkel was a duo he loved, and he was the one who introduced me to them. I could feel this hug throughout the rest of the song. When one of my friends looked at me to say something, she could see the tears streaming down my face, and my eyes softly closed and I was singing ever so slightly. His presence was there. That was one of the first times I felt a presence and trusted it. That trust has skyrocketed over the last ten years as I have worked to heal and grow. This moment allowed me to release a little of my grief, although it took until he was gone a full year for me to fully feel my grief.

The year following his passing was a whirlwind. I threw myself into doing anything and everything that could help my family after my brother's death. I would go to my parents' house at least once a week to try to help them through their grief. It took my mom one full month to speak to me; as soon as I walked into the house, she would start screaming at me to get out, that she didn't want to be around anyone. The first time she did that I was shocked. Mom was consumed by her anger while my dad went to the cemetery every day to talk to my brother. I did not focus on my own grief, and I didn't know how to come to terms that I would grow old without one of my siblings, so instead I focused on everyone and everything else.

I spent a lot of time with my sister-in-law. She asked me if I would talk to my brother's company about his benefits, and the company was willing to work with me. He had worked there for thirty years and was well liked. I worked with the company to understand all the benefits that would now go to his family and helped my sister-in-law with all that she needed. I met with the attorney to set up the education fund for the kids that we had decided to create. I set up the bank account and was the initial trustee of the account. I even sent out the thank you notes for the donations. I didn't grieve. I didn't allow any of my emotions to get in the way. I went back to work after a week. My colleagues on the business leadership team had a gift for me, a spa gift certificate. They were so very kind. I had amazing people around me to support me there, and I tried to act as if I was fine. I remember one of my co-workers once telling me that he was amazed at how great I was doing. All I could think was, *I'm acting buddy, I am falling apart inside.*

I let very few people know how I truly felt. I spent a lot of time with my family and let my personal life become my last priority. I would stop for a little visit on my way home from work, sometimes to my parents and sometimes to my sister-in-law. It was more than I had been doing prior to his death. During this time I spent more hours in my office, sometimes not getting home before 8pm. I had trouble sleeping and found myself up for hours many nights. I wanted to die if I'm being honest. *Losing me would have been so much easier on everyone else*, I would tell myself. That is how little I thought of me or my life compared to my brother. He was the firstborn, and we used to call him Mr. Perfect. He was a good son, father, husband, and friend; too many people were affected by his death. Mine would have been nothing. That sat on my heart for a very long time, but no one knew it. I would put my mask on every morning and wear it until I put my head on the pillow for bed.

During this time I didn't let myself feel. Food and shopping became the ways I filled voids. I couldn't feel anything, but on the outside I looked like I had it together. My mom even said that she was amazed by my ability to compartmentalize and still find joy in my life. I realized I had gained a lot of weight after his death and started Weight Watchers, again. I remember my first meeting with the leader, Amy. She asked me why I joined and I shared with the group that I recently lost my brother at the young age of fifty. Like me, he struggled with his weight most of his adult life. I didn't want to end up dead and knew I needed to lose weight. There was a woman next to me who hugged me when I said that and let me know how proud she was of me for sharing that. We became friends for quite a few years after that. I lost about twenty-five pounds, but even that didn't make me feel anything in particular. I just moved through life. In the past, losing that kind of weight would have made me feel sexy and caused me to look for men's attention. I was less inclined to do that this time.

Being the strong one has been a focal point of my life, and this focus intensified after my brother's death. My mom's fight to ensure I was independent helped me to be strong, and strength was something that the women in my extended family were proud of. I come from a line of strong women, so I used to put more pressure on myself to be like them. My grandmother, my mom's mom, attended the University of Warsaw in 1912, when women didn't go to school. She came to the United States with her mother and her infant son, following her husband who had left three months earlier. She had no idea if she would find him and or any of her family, she trusted that it would be okay. She and her husband began to build a life here, but her infant son died at two years old from Scarlet Fever, and they never really knew where he was buried due to how many children were being taken by Scarlet Fever and buried in groups.

Despite that unimaginable hardship, my grandparents became owners of a hardware store. They worked together and my great-grandmother cared for my mom and aunt once they were born. When my grandfather died suddenly in 1953, right after my oldest brother was born, my grandmother did not fall apart. She sold their business and moved back to the Bronx to be closer to her sisters. She still lived her life. She would visit us often, taking the bus from New York City. She traveled to Israel to meet a nephew she did not know she had. Her strength was admired by us all. Sometimes I wonder if my mom and I both were trying to be as strong as she was. Was the idea of the women having to be the strong ones conditioned in us, or was it in our DNA, or both?

I was strong after my first divorce. I kept it together and listened to "I Will Survive" by Gloria Gaynor as a way to remind me that I could get through anything. I was one of the first of my friends to go through a divorce and tried like hell to prove my worth and strength. I didn't need anyone, and I wanted everyone to know it. In fact, in 1998 when I decided to buy my house, I contacted a realtor and began to work with her without really telling anyone. I never brought my dad or my brothers to any of the houses I looked at, nor did I have them come with me when I decided to make an offer. My dad came with me the day of the inspection for my little modified Cape Cod style house in downtown Freehold. I remember him looking at my house and instead of saying something really positive and prideful, he said, "it's a little small." I immediately felt judged and compared myself to my brother as he had a four-thousand-square-foot house, and this one was about fourteen-hundred square feet. I looked right at my dad before speaking.

"I don't need a four-thousand-square-foot house, Dad, it's only me." Years later my dad would tell me how much he loved my house, the character it had, and the way I opened it up more and used the yard better. He actually loved it, coming over to help me put up shutters, and fixing things for me. He trusted my ninety-year-old neighbor to watch over me as well. I was proud of myself. I felt strong, and yet, that nagging comparison was always there, taunting me.

I moved on December 30th, it was an extremely cold day. My parents were at my new house with me, along with a friend and the movers. No matter what the movers did, they could not get my Queen sized mattress and boxspring for my bed upstairs. The hall and the stairwell were too narrow. It became obvious that I needed a split boxspring to get it upstairs. I had the movers put my bed in the spare bedroom and while they continued to bring things into my new house, I called 1-800-MATTRESS to order a new bed. In a matter of fifteen minutes I had a new bed and box spring being delivered in two days. Mom just looked at me in amazement.

"You got that done already?" she asked as she shivered in my new kitchen.

"Yes, it will be delivered on January 1st," I said like it was nothing.

"Wow, I would never have thought to make that phone call and get that done so fast," she said with such pride in her voice. "You really know how to get things done."

"I do Mom. I have to," I smiled but felt a heaviness in my chest.

"I'm so amazed by you." It was probably one of the nicest things Mom had ever said to me. She was never one to shower me with accolades, although I have been told that she regularly told others how proud she was of me. I had all the strength she admired, or so she told others.

Even though I used being strong as a defense mechanism for a long time, I don't want to downplay the importance of being strong, when needed. Strength can absolutely be positive. My strength and ability to get things done in a crisis was on display on September 11, 2001. I was working in Newark, New Jersey and was in a large meeting room early that morning. It was a beautiful, bright September day, with very little clouds against the bluest sky. As thirty of us sat in a meeting, someone came into the meeting room unannounced to share that a plane hit one of the twin towers. Being just outside of New York City, this was not a new phenomenon. There had been little planes and helicopters that had hit skyscrapers before. We had no idea what was happening. Fifteen minutes later, another person came in and told us a plane had hit the second tower. We knew at that moment that this was not an accident. We all got up and started back to our offices, trying to call people we knew who were working there, and checking on our teams. I ran to my boss's office.

We stood in silence watching what was happening on her television. I ran to my office and made sure my team was okay and that they had reached anyone they needed to reach. Within an hour, the company began to let people go home. I stayed and worked with the head of HR and my boss to help employees find hotel rooms if they couldn't get home, or car services and taxis if they usually took mass transit, as that was all shut down. I worked side by side with my boss until 3pm before going home.The drive home was the eeriest scene, like something out of a horror movie. The New Jersey Turnpike was empty, and all I could see was smoke rising from New York City. The strength it took to focus on getting people where they needed to be, hold space for those who were frightened, and realize that we were under an attack, was something that people counted on with me. I had broad shoulders, an ability to get things done, and a lot of problem solving skills. Sometimes strength is exactly what is needed.

My fortieth birthday was nine days after September 11th, and I decided to still host the small get together I had planned. People needed something to enjoy, and we needed to connect with each other. It was certainly a more subdued celebration than I had originally planned, but it allowed many of us to process what was happening through conversation, or forget about it for a while through partying and being present.

I was so excited to turn forty. I had success in my career, I now owned a lovely home in a downtown neighborhood, I could walk into my little town for breakfast, dinner, music, and fun, I had a yard I could begin to garden in, and a wonderful next door neighbor, Joe. Joe was a real farmer who grew and shared blueberries, tomatoes, corn, and beautiful flowers. Turning forty felt like I finally made it. It reminded me of the old Mary Tyler Moore show when she moved into the bigger apartment and hung up her M. It was her statement that she had made it. I felt like forty was that for me; a statement that I had made it. I had no idea what my forties had in store for me.

Sometimes my strength is needed, and sometimes it's a facade to keep me safe, or make me believe that I am safe. Fear helps me feel safe from my own emotions, safe from having to face myself, and safe from my feelings. Fear keeps me safe from being honest, and sometimes strength propels me into the role of fixer. Being a fixer is great when you are a problem solver like I am. The problem, though, is not everyone wants you to fix things for them. There have been times when, as the fixer, I stuck my nose into a place it didn't belong. When I was the fixer, it meant that I was always trying to take care of and control situations. Being a fixer sounds like a good enough role until you realize you are doing everything so that you don't have to face yourself, your fears, your trauma, or your wounds. And, of course, not everyone wants your help. Not everyone wants a fixer. My habit of fixing things developed mostly because of my own discomfort. If I wanted the situation changed, I believed I could be the one to change it, and that backfired on me many, many times throughout my life.

CHAPTER 7

Leading up to my fiftieth birthday, we found out that my niece, Stephanie, who was born with Down's Syndrome, had a brain tumor leaning on her brain stem. The brain stem is what shifted with my brother and caused him to be medically brain dead, and the idea that Stephanie now had something leaning on hers caused a lot of fear and concern for all of us. My lack of faith began to show itself to me. I wondered if I prayed if there was anyone who would listen.

My niece's surgery was scheduled three days after my fiftieth birthday. I was far from happy to be half a century old. I never expected to be celebrating this birthday without a partner by my side. I was miserable. I felt old, fat, and believed I was alone in the world. I kept wondering how I got to this point. Yes, I had a successful career and some terrific lifelong friends, but I felt completely alone. My milestone day was rightfully dwarfed by everything else going on, but one of my friends planned a dinner with some other friends for my birthday, a gesture I was grateful for. She shared the arrangements with me and an address. As I drove there, I realized that the restaurant chosen was one that my second husband and I frequented. It was one of our favorite spots. She said she made a mistake, and had thought she made the reservation elsewhere. Then she told me to just relax, that it would be fine. My anger came to the surface, and I was seething and ready to explode, although I tried to keep it in check. I was miserable to be there.

She tried to play it off, the realization of her choice hitting her. *How could she not realize it and make this reservation? How come I was so angry?* I sat with that for a while, and came to the conclusion that I wasn't important enough for her to consider my feelings. I was always questioning my worth, and assuming I didn't matter; I'm not loved or lovable, I would tell myself daily. This time though, I was beginning to notice how I felt and didn't like it. It was getting exhausting carrying that much anger, disappointment, shame, and guilt around.

I couldn't control what my niece was going through just like I couldn't control when my brother died. I felt helpless and had no faith in anything. I had no guidance to lean on, nothing to help me stay positive or understand that someone may listen to and answer a prayer. Because I had no faith in anything bigger than myself, I tried to control things including conversations. I used to play out conversations in my car, almost scripting them. For me, it was often about trying to find and be prepared with the words that would impact the other person the most. Only years later would I understand the victim mentality that I lived with, and how it showed up in those carefully planned conversations in my mind. I tried to control everything so I would not be the victim, yet I was playing the victim role often. I vacillated between anger and victimhood a lot, and the victim mentality definitely showed up in both of my marriages. With hindsight, I can see that I was always so afraid they would leave me, and I hung on so tight to those relationships, even when I was unhappy. I didn't learn the lesson that I needed to let go and trust until I was in my fifties.

Everything with my niece's surgery and my turning fifty was happening as I was trying to figure out why my second marriage imploded. I knew about his cheating, but I was trying to really reflect on me and us. An acquaintance from work also had a husband who cheated on her. During one of our many conversations she mentioned the book, *The Power of Now* by Eckart Tolle. That book began my quest. Just as I was reading it, I noticed that another woman I knew, Gina, was changing her career and trajectory. I met Gina when she was the executive director of a non-profit focused on helping women step into their power. Now she was going to become a "happiness advocate," advising and coaching on spirituality. It seemed like divine timing to me and I reached out to her. That began a multiple-year relationship with Gina as my spiritual advisor and coach. Therapy had helped me with the basics, understanding that I could reframe thoughts so they weren't so negative, but Gina helped me to find my faith which took my healing to a new level.

Through her readings that included tarot card pulls, and our discussions around her knowledge of energy, Gina poured herself into me and helped me to begin to understand there was a greater force at play. She helped me with releasing judgments of myself and understanding that I was wallowing in shame. It was not on the surface, but my fear of taking on more shame was certainly at the root of my trying to control situations by being a people pleaser and a fixer. Gina was fantastic at seeing the signs that I was missing, and she was so good at pointing out those coincidences that really were God Winks, and not coincidences at all.

"They are there to show you that you are being guided, you are on the right path," she said to me one day during a session. I was telling her about a family of deer I had seen while I was out on a walk the day prior. I was deep into my role as a fixer as there was some major family drama happening at the time, causing rifts between everyone. I was convinced that it was not only my duty, but my superpower, to fix things, especially in my family. As the only one of my siblings without children or a spouse at the time, I believed it should all land on my shoulders.

"How many deer were there?" Gina asked.

"It looked like a mama with four of her babies," I said, and she giggled. *What's so funny?* I didn't even connect the dots that I had been stressed about my sister-in-law and her four children; I wanted to have a deeper connection with them and felt lost on how to achieve it.

"You saw those deer on your walk yesterday because the Universe wants you to know that they are okay. That's the first message. The second message is that they want to reconnect with you, too." I shrugged it off as coincidence at the time, because I wasn't far enough into my spiritual awakening to accept and receive this message. I chose to believe it meant nothing, but questioned my own beliefs when, just a few days later, my sister-in-law called me just to talk. *Maybe there really was something to this spirituality thing.*

During one of my sessions with Gina, she asked me, "How do you want to show up in the world?" I was never asked that question before. It was always about what did I want to do, what did I want to accomplish, but never how did I want to show up. That shift in energy changed everything for me. I no longer focused on what I wanted to do but more about how I want to approach the situation. She had me read a lot of books including *You Can Heal Your Life* by Louise Hay, *Change Your Thoughts - Change Your Life* by Dr. Wayne Dyer, and *The Law of Attraction* by Esther and Jerry Hicks. She helped me to see the signs and guidance from the Universe and to begin to hear my inner wisdom. It would be years later, through consistent meditation, that my inner wisdom became a dominant force in guiding me. It had been for so long, but I felt forced in corporate America to abandon it. I had to prioritize data and statistics over my intuition. With Gina's help, I started to believe a bit more in my intuition. I started to listen to it a bit more.

Through Louise Hay's work, I started to use affirmations to help me change my mindset. One day I went to a friend's house and noticed she had put Post-Its all over her bathroom mirror with affirmations on them. They said things like, "You are beautiful," "You are kind," and "You are loved." She had young daughters, and they had placed similar notes on their mirrors too. It made me so happy to see young women receiving validation like that, and I thought it was completely brilliant, so I decided to add positive affirmations to my bathroom mirror, too. *It was such an easy way to remind myself of how far I had come, and how far I could still go if I just believed in myself,* I thought. But when I got home with my Post-Its and colorful markers, I couldn't think of anything to write. Absolutely nothing came to me. Each time I thought about something to write, my mind would try to talk me out of it. It took me a full month before I could write affirmations and put them on my mirror. Once I was able to write them, and I started to believe them, I noticed small shifts starting to happen. The notes said things like, "I am worthy of my own love and affection," "I am lovable, I am loving and I am loved," and "Self-love is first love," and I would feel a little better each time I saw them.

When writing affirmations, you want to be clear to write what you want, always in the positive. You want to write them as if they are happening now, not in the future. Use positive words, never 'but' or 'try'. As you write them for the first time, know that you may start to hear your inner voice convincing you that you are not worthy of these thoughts. That is your inner critic. My best advice is 1) pay attention to what it is telling you, this is great awareness for your healing, growth and transformation journey; and 2) tell your critic "thank you for being here and trying to protect me. I do not need that protection. I am going to sit you beside me to work with me."

These stayed on my mirror for years. Of course they had to be rewritten over time, and I added some and removed some as needed. Over time, though, this process helped me to focus more on the positive and was one more step in my healing. At this time, I also began to use Louise Hay's Mirror Work methodology that I still share with my clients today. As a practice, stand at a mirror, and really look deeply into your own eyes. No judgment. As you look into your eyes, tell yourself, "I love you." "I adore you." "You are the most important person in my life."

Once I started doing affirmations and nurturing myself, even if it was just a little bit of time spent each day, I began to realize that Corporate America brought out my masculine energy. The entire system is built by masculine energy and values it; decisiveness, execution oriented, externally focused, predictable, logical, risk taking, goal setting, standing up for yourself. All important, however, so out of balance. It is the reason that the number one normalized emotion for men in corporate environments is anger. They are considered passionate when they show anger. A woman who portrays that same anger is seen as a bitch and too emotional. The system keeps everyone that is in it out of balance. The lack of balance leads to the idea that compassion or empathy is weakness, and it makes it easy for women in corporate America to question their decisions. Yet those were the best leaders I worked with, the ones who could balance inspiration and compassion with competitiveness and execution. Very few could, and the ones who could were usually women.

I realized I no longer wanted to feel all that anger, all that predictability. I wanted to be softer. I started to read more about both masculine and feminine energy. Some of the attributes of the feminine that I wanted to really tap into were my intuition as well as creativity. I knew embracing both of those traits would help me approach my life with more authentic joy. I needed more flow and less structure. The daily grind was definitely getting to me. One of the outlets for my creativity and intuition became writing. My journal entries became a little longer and deeper and I realized that I wanted to write more. I wanted to write a children's book, and perhaps my story as well. I knew there were parts of me that I wanted to share in order to help other women going through similar things. Just as I was beginning to explore how I could use my feminine energy more, a writing retreat was placed in front of me. I saw a post on Facebook on a friend's page. Another woman tagged my friend in a post regarding a writing and travel retreat in Italy for later that year. I clicked on the link and began to read. "Travel is an incredible way to awaken your creativity!" Well, that seemed like quite the sign!

I reached out to my friend to find out what I could about the people running the retreat. My friend was not going to go, however, she gave a glowing recommendation for the person organizing the trip. In October of 2013, I spent seven glorious days on the Ligurian coast outside of Genoa with a group of aspiring writers and all-around-amazing women. This trip really opened me up, both to my own gifts and to the camaraderie of women I did not know. I remember saying to friends the night before I left that I was going to leave the current version of Suzy home. I was going to go there not being the woman with two failed marriages, or a dead sibling, or parents who expected me to hold it all together. I didn't want to be labeled as the fixer or the go-getter while I was there, I just wanted to connect with feminine energy.

During my layover in Munich, I connected with two of the women who were also attending, and we flew to Genoa together. The three of us took a cab to the boutique hotel where the retreat was being held. Melissa was an accountant from Scottsdale who I clicked with immediately. We decided to put our bags in our rooms and take a walk on the Passeggiata, a gorgeous promenade that trailed the seawall. We walked and talked, meandering in and out of gardens and then back onto the passeggiata. We found a beautiful outdoor cafe and sat for a drink. Immediately, the server came over with a small bowl of nuts, a small bowl of chips, and olives. This was something we weren't prepared for; everywhere in Italy you receive a little snack when you sit down to drink or eat. It is a beautiful custom.

We each ordered a vodka drink and continued getting to know each other. By the time we left the cafe, Melissa knew I was divorced twice and lost my brother. *There goes my "different version of Suzy" plan,* I judged myself as we finished our meal. Her reaction lacked judgement, and was instead filled with compassion, and I realized then that this was a part of me. Acting like these things didn't happen to me didn't make sense. What I had to do was not let them define me, which is what I was feeling when I planned to not share that part of me. The trip validated that writing was a real creative outlet for me, and that I had impactful stories to tell. Being with a group of women for a week let me really revel in the feminine energy I was so lacking in my day-to-day back home. We surrendered ourselves to the retreat guides, going where they brought us. We did something new each day, whether that be a cooking class or a trip to Portofino. We traveled by train all around the area and played fun creative games. I had to get a picture with a focaccia baker while we were in Portofino and then write about the experience. The first bakery I walked into, I was thrown out of just as quickly. The baker would not allow me to take a picture and would not even talk with me. I strolled into a second bakery. I was looking around and spotted a beautiful tray of fresh baked focaccia bread. I asked if I could take a picture of the bread with the baker.

"You American?" the baker asked me.

"Yes, I am."

"New York?"

"No, New Jersey!" I smiled.

"It's the same, come here," the baker said, motioning me behind the counter. She was so full of life, and her energy was so fun. She gave me a huge hug after we took the picture together, and sent me on my way with a huge piece of the fresh focaccia bread. It was such a special moment; this woman was a complete stranger, but her energy made me feel right at home, and I remember thinking to myself that I wanted more of that energy in my life.

While I was in Italy, changes were occurring in the human resources organization at my company back home. I received a call from my leader letting me know that two of my colleagues were being promoted to the next level, Vice President, and I was not. I believed my role was equal, yet the company did not.

"When I share with my peers how you excel in your role," he started to explain, "they tell me it's because you have been in the distribution business a long time. They need to see you elsewhere to believe you are as good as I say. When you return, we will talk, I have an idea."

"But Mary has been in her role equally as long and she is being promoted."

"Yes but her role is much more complex," he said, and I couldn't argue with that. I felt frustrated and overlooked. I went into a victim mentality, my comfort zone, and started placing blame on him for ruining my trip. I went to bed angry that night, and felt the familiar wave of disappointment and helplessness wash over me. *Why am I always second? I am never, ever chosen first...what's wrong with me?* I woke up still upset. I decided to take a long walk on the passeggiata before breakfast. I wrote about this walk during a writing exercise that evening:

> *The ferocity of the sea paralleled the feelings in my soul. Unrest.*
>
> *I could feel the sea spray on my skin with each crash of a wave on the jagged rocks below.*
>
> *The scene reminded me of the many books and movies where the heroine decided the world was more cruel than the rolling deep and leapt to her demise. Was I that heroine? Was I beyond ending my pain? Was this pain so bad that I needed to end it?*
>
> *I was so out of sorts. I felt alone and dark. Again, I wasn't good enough. Again, I wasn't enough.*
>
> *As I enjoyed the passeggiata listening to the roar of the water below, an Italian man probably in his seventies caught my eye. He was wearing a lemon yellow jacket and wire rimmed glasses. Unlike many before him, he wore a smile and not the scowl you see on so many. He looked at me."Caio Bella!" he said as his face broke into a smile that was warm like sunshine. At that moment, the weight of my evening woes, of my disappointment and my anger were lifted.*
>
> *He will never know how much I needed that. He will never know that on that dark morning, he shed light on me and kept me moving forward.*

The sea was no longer ferocious.

This interaction, as brief as it was, allowed me to lift my veil of shame and disappointment. This man reminded me that I was enough. I was more than the promotion or the role. The entire retreat gave me a boost I needed. I had such fun writing during that entire week. I had never been with a group of writers before and enjoyed everyone's writing. I caught myself a few times comparing myself with others, and I had to continue to remind myself that this was not a competition. Competition was what I knew. I was conditioned to be competitive. My family was a big sports family. My parents first official date was a boxing match, they were both big fans of that sport. I played softball as a kid, and we all watched everything. Being competitive was all I really knew. That competition drove me often, but it also held me back. I knew I was looking for the pat on the back, to be considered one of the better writers. I wasn't; I was average. However, I could tell a story and that was what the retreat helped me to see.

On the first day of the retreat, we were each asked to pick a rock from a pile and grab a Sharpie. We were instructed to think about what we wanted to release or let go of and write it on the rock. The objective was to continue to write on the rock during the week as we discovered new things about ourselves that we wanted to release. My rock had words on it like control, failure, victim, and lack of trust written all over it. On the last day of the retreat, we threw the rocks into the ferocious sea. It was magical. We had prosecco and cried, letting the emotional release happen without resistance. When our week was over, I realized that I left some of the heaviness of my identity, my grief, anger, and judgement, in that sea. I still struggled with these things, but it all felt lighter and more manageable.

Once again, I started the process of evolving, of having the breakthrough, and didn't carry through with my progress once I was back home. I did continue to write more after this trip, though. I started my blog, The Morning Butterfly, at the very end of 2014, which has been an amazing outlet for me in many ways. It has allowed me to explore my journey and help others see they are not alone. It has also allowed me to express myself differently and enhance my writing. In fact, I printed the first two blog posts and brought them to my mom. She read them both intently and looked up at me. "I could have written these," she said. "I know." I replied. And just like that we knew how alike we were and how much I absorbed. My blog was my first foray into writing vulnerably.

Like everything though, it was another thing added to my plate. My life was busy. It was hard to integrate everything I was learning to achieve my big breakthrough. I had a lot of little breakthroughs for a very long time, and always went back to the comfort of familiarity; I would always lean back into being self-effacing, feeling disappointed and unworthy, people-pleasing, and avoiding my feelings, and of course eating my way through many of those emotions.

I was promoted mid-2014 to a bigger business in the company. I spent the last three and a half years of my time with the firm in this role. Gina asked me what type of leader I wanted to be when I moved to this role, and I told her I wanted to be open-hearted. We spent time working through what being open-hearted looked like to me, and how I was going to show up as a leader in that energy. I knew that anger had driven me before, and didn't want that at all. I also knew that in my last role, I had factions on my team and there was a lot of competition that I did not want. I wanted to be as transparent with the team as possible, and I wanted to lead with compassion, empathy, and my heart. The team didn't always make that easy, however, over time we created a great working relationship. Once some changes were made the team began to gel.

That open-heart approach was about how they viewed me, and how I led with compassion. It certainly wasn't that they would get to know me. I kept a lot to myself. My heart was not nearly as open as I pretended it to be. I really didn't let people in fully. As I continued to learn about and lean into my feminine energy more, I realized that for a long time I stayed busy so I wouldn't have to feel anything. The number one way I began to understand feminine energy and balancing it with my masculine energy was by slowing down. Masculine energy is action oriented, and all about being the doer. Feminine energy is intuitive and creative, it is more about just being. As I started to slow down a bit by meditating and spending more time in nature where I could be completely present and at ease, I started to notice that I could hear and feel my intuition more. It was less about letting others do for me and more about not needing to do for them to feel worthy. I lived so much in my masculine energy, doing for others, being assertive, being logical that I stopped trusting my intuition. I focused too much on needing to do things on my own to feel validated and worthy.

Gina helped me tap into my feminine energy. She taught me that "just being" wasn't lazy, it was necessary. She left me with a lesson I want to pass onto you. You cannot always go, go, go, you must sit in silence and allow yourself to feel. You need to feel all of your feelings, then take a step toward whatever action aligns with what you desire. Being in stillness allows your inner wisdom to come forth and be heard, and embracing your inner wisdom is crucial for healing that actually lasts.

EXERCISE:

Sit comfortably on a chair, feet firmly on the ground. Have a journal or paper and pen nearby. Allow your shoulders to relax. Let your jaw relax and begin to breathe slowly. When you are ready, either close or lower your eyes.

Ask yourself: what does masculine energy look and feel like in my body? And wait to see what comes up, no judgment. When you are ready, ask yourself, what does feminine energy look and feel like in my body? And wait again to see what comes up. Allow yourself to see or hear or feel whatever happens. After a few moments, slowly open your eyes and capture whatever you saw in your journal.

Let this begin your journey to understanding how things feel in your body. Allow yourself to learn about these energies and which you may use more. And give yourself so much grace through this. Remember, this journey is for our lifetime, there is no rush.

CHAPTER 8

Suzy, that dress looks amazing on you!" It was a Monday morning and I was sporting a pretty wrap dress I found at the mall over the weekend. I said thank you, but I didn't receive the compliment. I started talking down to myself instead. *If they saw the back of the dress they would see how fat you actually look in it. They were just saying that to be nice.* And then I interrupted myself, fighting against those nasty thoughts. *Why can't you just accept a compliment, Suzy? What's wrong with you?* All I kept thinking about during the day was how I sound when I talk to myself. *I sound like Mom,* I thought. I was constantly picking myself apart. *Why do I always treat myself as if I am my own worst enemy?* I realized I was always focused on my flaws, and because of that, when anything didn't go the way I hoped, I found fault in myself.

It was always because I wasn't good enough, pretty enough, fun enough, thin enough, smart enough...fill in the blank. I didn't talk to myself the way I spoke to the people I loved, that was for sure. My inner-critic was all about judgment and fear. And what I have learned is that all judgment is in some way a projection of something within us. Simply put, all judgment is self-judgment. And self-judgment keeps us down, at a low energy frequency, where possibilities and opportunity may escape us. Releasing all of that judgment and no longer comparing ourselves with anyone except ourselves is one of the staples in healing. I have found that releasing all of that judgment of myself allows me to see who I am, and become who and what I want to become.

Let's try an exercise here to help you truly see your self-talk, labels and judgment. I will give you a prompt, you write down the first thing that pops into your head:

Prompt	**Internal Monologue**
You are running out the door and catch a glimpse of yourself in the mirror	
You just realized you made a colossal mistake at work	
You just lost your temper with your partner	
You have been asked to speak in front of a group you do not know well	

For many of us, our first reaction to ourselves is rarely positive. We look for our so-called flaws. We look for ways to beat ourselves down all in the effort to become better. We know that positive reinforcement actually changes behavior, not negative reinforcement. Negative reinforcement will beat us into compliance for a while, but never really changes anyone's behavior. Our views of ourselves have been created over time. It isn't just our physical being we judge, we judge every part of ourselves that we don't feel is good enough.

We are conditioned to be competitive. In order to be truly competitive we learn to compare ourselves to everyone. Comparison is one of the roots of judgment, self-criticalness, and the limits we place on ourselves. It's rare people are rooting for others as well as themselves. Most think there is a finite amount of prosperity and abundance and therefore don't want others to get as much as them. When I had no faith in anything bigger, I thought my grit was all I needed. I thought that to be competitive I had to look at what was wrong with me and right with the others. I always knew they couldn't outwork me. That was my go to if I thought I wasn't as good as someone else. We tend to compare our entire existence with what we see of another's life. We have no concept that they may be feeling all that we feel. This conditioning starts young, whether at home with parents asking one child to be more like their sibling or in school with grades. Let's not get started on the conditioning of girls to compare their bodies to those that the fashion industry has deemed perfect, beautiful, etc. That is some of the worst conditioning and comparisons there are. The damage is far reaching.

As we begin the journey of unraveling our habits, our go-to's, our actions/inactions and patterns of behavior, we need to release judgment. Our reflection and awareness needs to be honest and not shame-filled. This isn't a time to beat yourself up, it is a time of understanding. It is a time to look at all you uncover with love, compassion and empathy; or as I say, give yourself grace and space. Grace to fully love yourself as you face some realities about the hurt you feel, the disappointment you have endured and the stories you have told yourself. Space to allow yourself to embrace all of you, to release the pent-up emotion and hear your inner wisdom.

Giving up comparison and judgment is far from easy in a culture that thrives on comparison and competitiveness. It takes work. It takes patience. You will find yourself going along feeling good about the lack of judgment and how much happier you are with yourself and then boom! A judgment crosses your mind. Once you do become aware of your judgments, you will begin to actually stop them in your brain. More importantly, these judgments allow you to go deeper in your healing, understanding the depths of your conditioning and then deciding how you want to feel and who you want to be. All judgment is a projection of unrealized trauma, or other behavior within you. To put it simply, all judgment is self-judgment. That judgment energy keeps us so small and low in energetic frequency. It may give us a feeling that we are better than others, such a fleeting feeling. Why do we feel the need to be better? It's all conditioning.

My decision to retire from corporate America occurred after my mom's death. In those weeks following, I was dealing with her death, my dad's hospitalization which was followed by him moving in with me for a while, and then the end of my thirty-five year career. I also saw a friendship that I thought could be more falling by the wayside, without understanding why. Honestly, it felt like the end of any identity I knew. I realized I needed to clear my head. I asked my brother and sister-in-law if I could stay at their condominium in Naples, Florida and once they said yes, I made a plan to drive to Florida myself. I had never driven the one-thousand miles to Florida by myself, and I was excited about the adventure. My dad was not. He was convinced that I was going to be kidnapped.

"I don't understand why you can't just fly down and get there," he said one night over dinner.

"I want to clear my head Dad, the drive down and the adventure in doing it myself will help me do that. What are you so worried about?" I asked.

"I know you. You are going to stop somewhere for something to eat, have a drink. You're going to start telling people your life story because that is what you do and someone is going to figure out you are alone. Next thing, they are going to kidnap and murder you." I stood there in disbelief.

"You watch too much true crime TV!" I said, "I promise, I won't stop at a bar and I won't tell anyone my life story. I need to do this." And I did. I planned it all out, and set off on my solo road trip.

I brought a copy of Gabby Bernstein's *Judgment Detox* with me to read while I was in Florida. I read her stories intently, seeing some of my judgment clearly. Then she added an exercise. I decided to do the exercise for five days and not read the book again until I had completed the five days. The exercise was a way to understand the depths of your judgments and how they always point to something going on within you. On day one of her exercise I had over forty judgments on my piece of paper. What hit me hard was the depths of my self-criticalness. Did I really think that poorly of myself? It was clear that I had no trust or faith in myself. I basically ripped myself apart through judging others.

Gabby's exercise and book helped me to really release that criticalness that I was so fond of. That also allowed me to really stop a lot of the self-deprecating humor, although that pops up from time to time. If you are at a point where you would like to get honest with yourself, you will need to drop judgment. Here is the exercise from Gabby that I modified a bit:

Make three columns on a sheet of paper. The titles of each column should be written on top and I would suggest doing this exercise for a minimum of five days. Allow yourself to really go deep on what it is about you that made the judgments okay. Perhaps take some time after you fill out your grid each night to journal and see what emotions may come up for you.

Write all your judgments down	What made those judgments okay? (rationalization)	What is it about me that made those judgments okay?

When you ask yourself the last question, be honest. In order to be honest, you may need to dig a little deeper, don't accept the first response if it isn't deep enough. Nobody else needs to see this and you can toss it when you are done. It is a great way to become hyper-aware of all the judgments you make in a day about yourself. It is a great way to begin your self-healing journey. You must become aware of your patterns of behavior, action and inaction, and be super honest with yourself to heal. In order to do all of that, you must stop judging yourself.

Becoming hyper aware of your judgments allows you to change, to heal, and to understand how you are projecting onto others. Had I learned this earlier, perhaps I would not have emotionally bled so much on both of my husbands and marriages. Perhaps there would have been less heartache and more love in each marriage. Freeing yourself of those judgments opens your heart. It opens your heart to love, and most of all it opens your heart to self-love.

One of the ways we can create the space we need to hear our inner wisdom is meditation. Meditation is a lifelong practice, and did not come naturally to me. I mentioned my first time to Miraval in 2003. This was the first time I had practiced meditation. As I was working with Gina around 2014, Deepak Chopra was recording twenty-one-day meditation challenges with Oprah Winfrey. I was a fan of each of them. Deepak's voice always relaxed me and I loved that he practiced both Eastern and Western medicine and tried to find ways to bridge them both. Oprah was a self-made woman with an incredibly difficult past. I loved her honesty and gumption. Together, they helped me to create a meditation practice that led me to approaching life differently. The more I practiced, the better I began to feel. I started to realize that I felt calmer, and I wasn't as quick to react. I also started to really see patterns of behavior that I wanted to change.

After I retired, I decided to take a Deepak Chopra course in meditation. The first course was to learn about meditation and receive my own mantra. Deepak and his team worked with Yogis as well as ancient transcripts from India to resurrect Primordial Sound Mantra meditation. I received a sanskrit mantra based upon the sound of the universe the moment I was born. This vibration allowed me to go back to the moments before all of the conditioning kicked in. I began to realize that my soul needed to be awakened. My authenticity needed to be awakened. The stories and the narratives needed to be changed.

There are one-hundred-and-eight sanskrit mantras. The mantras don't have meaning, they are used for vibrational sound. In that way, the mantras do not immediately trigger a thought, thus, allowing you to have a gap between thoughts, the gap of infinite possibilities. This was a game changer for me. It allowed my brain to finally slow down enough for me to see patterns of behavior, understand actions and begin to think more intentionally. Now I was excited. When I started to see that this meditation was helping me see myself honestly and hear my inner wisdom more, I knew others could benefit. I signed up to become certified in this type of meditation. That training concluded just before my dad passed away. I was able to tell him I was now a certified meditation teacher. He was so proud. He had lived with me on and off over the year that I was in training. He saw the effort I put in and he saw the differences in my behavior. The anger lessened. The sadness lifted. Meditation has helped me move from looking at life through a lens of fear to looking at life through a lens of love.

Meditation is a tool that will help you to start to see the patterns in your behavior, action and inaction. Stillness and quiet allows us to hear the inner wisdom and intuition. It allows us to connect to a powerful source, whether you call that God, the Universe or your higher power. Without meditation, the seven weeks my dad was in the hospital prior to his death would have been much harder to navigate. It was the height of the Covid pandemic and I could not be in the hospital. The doctors were overwhelmed, as were the nurses. I couldn't get people on the phone, and I didn't know what was happening.

There were many times when all I could do was meditate so I would remain calm. There were days where I would meditate five times a day. All you ever need in order to meditate is a comfortable and safe place to sit with your eyes lowered or closed. You don't need anything special. In fact, the best way to begin is with five minutes of stillness each morning. Below is a quick way to begin this practice. I would suggest setting an alarm for a few minutes and allow yourself to be. I always suggest having a journal or notepad around when you do this, you never know what you may want to capture as you come back. And sometimes, those realizations happen later. As Deepak Chopra says, "we do not meditate to become great meditators. We do it to evolve our soul and become enlightened."

Here is a simple, five-minute meditation that can help you get started. It will work whether you read through and follow the steps, or listen to it here: suzydomenick.com/meditations

Steps:

1. Sit comfortably on a chair or cross-legged on the floor. Allow your spine to be straight, as energy flows more freely through a straight spine.
2. Roll your shoulders back and away from your ears; allow your arms to relax in your lap and when you are ready, gently lower or close your eyes.
3. Begin to notice your breath. As you notice your breath, begin to deepen it. On the inhale, fill your belly, let your ribs expand and your chest rise. Then slowly exhale all that air out.
4. Again, inhale deeply, fill your belly, ribs expand, chest rise and again let it all out. One more deep breath, and then exhale. Allow yourself to relax into your breath, with each breath relax your shoulders, your back, your hips.
5. Imagine a bright white light on the crown of your head. Feel that light soften and relax the crown of your head. Feel that light across your forehead, around your eyes, your cheeks, your jaw, around your mouth and let your face relax letting your tongue float to the bottom of your mouth. Imagine that light starting on your left shoulder, around your neck to your right shoulder, letting your shoulders get heavy and falling away from your ears. Feel that light on your upper back, your middle back, your low back, letting all those muscles soften and relax.

6. Feel that light on your upper arms, your elbows, your forearms, your wrists, your hands and your fingers, letting your arms get heavy in your lap and let all the tension flow out of them.
7. Feel that light across your chest and belly, letting all those muscles soften and relax.
8. Feel that light around your hips and glutes letting those muscles soften and go more deeply into whatever is supporting you.
9. Feel that light around your thighs and hamstrings, your knees, your calves and your shins, your ankles, your feel and your toes. Let your legs get heavy as if they are melting into the floor below.
10. Feel that light wrap around your entire body, let it hold you, soften you, relax you.
11. I invite you to bring your attention to the center of your chest, to your heart center and let that light fill you up, with appreciation, compassion, gratitude, happiness, joy, love. Let those emotions wash over you.
12. Continue breathing as you silently say, Om, as you breathe, in and out, slowly and steadily. When your alarm goes off, wiggle your toes and your fingers and bring yourself slowly back to your body. Then slowly open your eyes and begin your day.

CHAPTER 9

Back in January 2016 I read this quote and wrote about it for my blog: "Sometimes it is not that people change, it's just that the mask falls off." The entry was called "The Mask." As I shared in the blog post, this made me realize there were other ways to look at what happened with my second husband. We divorced after five or so years of marriage, and for a long time I wondered what really happened. Did he change or did his mask fall off? He hid his insecurities, even to himself. He wore a mask of a man of confidence and a bit of swagger and even arrogance. The guy under the mask was filled with demons and deep self-doubt. I realize now that he and I both went into our relationship with a mask on; I was trying to pretend that I was fully healed from my first marriage, and believed that I was the best version of myself when he met me. But in reality, the anger was still there, the self-doubt and the lack of self-worth...it was all still there. *But I have a partner, so I'm fine,* I would tell myself time and time again. I was relying on him to make my life whole, and now I recognize that I am responsible for making my life whole on my own, and allowing a partner to enhance it.

That quote gave me the inspiration to really think about the masks we all wear. The masks may hide parts of ourselves that we do not like. There is the mask of always being busy, that way we avoid feeling much. The mask of acting like we love someone, only to never really do anything for them to feel that love. The mask of confidence to hide just how insecure we are about our abilities. The mask of happiness so people don't see the sadness, anger or grief underneath. His mask covered that he was focused on what he could get in return. He was a taker although his mask made you believe he would give you the shirt off his back. When I was depressed and couldn't fill his cup anymore, he had no patience. He needed to have someone fill his cup, he was not capable of filling it himself.

What I have realized after years of healing, growth, and always transforming, is we do all have masks. Those masks come from the stories we have told ourselves, the beliefs we hold and the conditioning we have about ourselves and society. We all hide parts of ourselves and often from people who we profess we love. Most of all though, we wear masks and hide parts of ourselves to ourselves. We convince ourselves that our patterns of behavior are just the way we are. We believe that we can't change, we have been this way forever. We believe that we don't need to feel emotions, bypass them. Act like everything is okay.

I was the Queen of "I'm fine." I tried like hell to not let people know what was going on inside of me. I wore that mask as a way to hide my fear. I also sometimes wore that mask knowing a person would poke through and know I wasn't ok. That made me feel important to that person and I needed that. I didn't always feel very important in people's lives. I'm not sure I ever realized that. I felt bypassed. Almost as if people just assumed I was fine because I always acted fine. I do have one friend who seems to know when I'm not and shows up without thinking about it. She moved into my house when my brother died. She looked at me and said, "I'm not letting you go through this alone, you tell me what to do and I will do it." I would not have gotten through the week after his death and his funeral without her living in my house. She often knows when I have a mask on.

We also have a mask that everyone knows we are reliable and counts on us. It may have been the mask that gave us the success in our life that we looked for. Given it worked to get the success, why would I change it now? Change only comes when you are in discomfort. I knew my mask was not the authentic me. I no longer wanted to be the heroine and be there for everyone else. I no longer wanted to feel second. I needed to make myself first. I no longer wanted to feel the grief, the sadness, the anger. I wallowed in it for longer than I wanted to admit, although on the outside you didn't see that. When I went on disability for a month at work, people were shocked. I remember talking to my boss about taking the leave.

"Suzy, do what you need to do to feel better. Please know though that I am not seeing any balls drop." His tone was sincere.

"Of course not," I said with a small smile, "My team is catching them. Trust me, I'm dropping them." I needed this disability. This was right after my second husband moved out after the private investigator. I couldn't think straight even though I appeared fine. My niece had just graduated from college and we were at her graduation party when I told my parents that my doctor was putting me on disability for one month so I could focus on my mental health. My mother looked over at me with a horrified look on her face.

"Don't do that! They will fire you! And don't tell them why!" Her scarcity mindset was front and center. She was fearful on my behalf. She was concerned that my mental health would make them question me as an employee. My brother intervened.

"She can go on disability, Mom, they aren't going to fire her." My parents were convinced that you never tell your boss that you have mental health issues, and companies fire people who don't work twenty-four-seven.

The month was the best thing I could have done. I saw my therapist, my psychiatrist, and took a week and went back to Miraval. I had deep tissue massages, one-on-one sessions with healers, worked with the horses again, and really allowed myself to feel all of my feelings. By feeling them, I could get back to a place where I could thrive, not just survive. My masks started to dwindle a little.

Shoving our emotions aside only keeps us holding onto them longer. We hold on to them tightly when we over-think and over-control them. And we hold onto them physically, in our cells. According to Deepak Chopra, more than eighty percent of diseases, he believes, are caused by chronic inflammation and lifestyle choices. One of the culprits of chronic inflammation is too much cortisol and adrenaline in our bodies.These two hormones are prevalent when we are in our survival body or fight, flight, freeze, fawn. Many of us spend many hours per day sitting in our survival body. The pressure we feel from deadlines and life tends to keep us in our sympathetic nervous system more than our body was meant to be. Our cells suck these two stress hormones up and by not releasing our emotions and allowing ourselves to always be pressurized, our body becomes inflamed. Couple that with smoking, excessive drinking, not enough exercise or sunshine, too much processed foods, obesity, etc, and you have the recipe for many illnesses.

After I retired and gave up the fifty and sixty-hour work weeks and the two-hour commutes, I noticed changes in my body. I could actually feel my body move differently, and behave differently. I saw the puffiness in my face begin to subside. I was losing that chronic inflammation. Every person I talk with who left corporate America feels this change. I also spent a lot of time in the beginning of my retirement with my cousin, Shari, an incredibly gifted intuitive healer. Shari had been like a sister to me and we had gone through a lot together. She is one of the safest people in my life. Never judgmental and always filled with love, she was one person I told everything to. She was helping me heal through my time after my second marriage, connecting to my little girl, and finding my authentic self.

Connecting with my little girl or inner child was incredible for me. It was the first time I started to realize that she was the one who never felt loved or accepted or wanted. She was who I needed to heal. She was helping me gain faith. She was helping me find faith in new and different ways of being. I needed to have faith that adult me could love child me the way she needed; faith that adult me understood child me was always enough. I needed to have faith beyond me as well. Using practices that were new to me, from meditation to tapping, to spending time in sacred circles where angels and guides shared their wisdom, all helped me realize faith. Shari introduced me to many of these modalities. As Gina and Shari shared their gifts with me, they both started to show me my gifts.

My intuition was really very strong when I trusted myself. Many times I would disregard the feeling I had about someone because of my lack of trust. My ability to read a situation or a person was actually my intuition, I didn't know that. I thought I was being observant, hyper-analytical, or it was just a coincidence. So often in my life, I seemed to be on the brink of a breakthrough. Whether that be after my first divorce, when I went to Japan, or my first time at Miraval, I seemed poised to really understand myself and begin to heal. Very often, I didn't feel authentic. I thought I was supposed to be a certain way so I showed up that way. I was supposed to be tough, that's what everyone wanted. If I was soft, if I showed my emotion, I was considered weak. My authenticity came through in my care for others. Although at times I put others way ahead of my own hopes and desires, my care was real. My loyalty was real. My love for others was real. My need to please, my need to control, my lack of boundaries, and my fear of people leaving me was not real. Those dictated the way I reacted to things. Those feelings were because of the narratives I played in my head. I always felt as if I had to prove my worth over and over.

I did retire from corporate America in early 2018, but I knew I would continue to work, both because I wanted some income and because I saw that working later into life helps the brain to stay sharp. Both my parents worked until they were eighty, and both had sharp brains just about to the end of their lives. Coaching was always a part of my role in human resources. I was coaching leaders of all levels from the first role I had in Macy's until I left Prudential. I had been certified in Stakeholder Centered Coaching while I was in my job. This was a great coaching program that was focused on executives. It focused on solutions and behavior that was potentially a detriment for the executive. It was never focused on the whole person. I knew that I wanted to coach and I knew that it wasn't executive coaching in a company that excited me. I wanted to help others heal, grow and transform. I decided on a coaching program through iPEC (Institute for Professional Excellence in Coaching).

This program helped me transform even more than the work I had already done on myself. The growth that came out becoming a certified coach was dramatic. The breakthroughs kept coming. As I was being coached by my peer group and peer coaches, I was seeing myself through different eyes. I saw how I took things that occurred so personally, as if I was the cause of everything or it was to hurt me. I internalized events and made them about me. By internalizing things and making it about me, I responded from a place of being a victim. The anger or sadness, the frustration all came from thinking that I was the cause of or reason for whatever occurred.

One of the greatest tools introduced was the Energy Leadership Index Assessment. Unlike other assessments that I am certified in, this was not about hard wiring. This was much more subjective. It was like getting feedback that you could use to create sustainable change. It was through this assessment that my victimhood really stood out for me. As I was learning about my tendencies, I was also going through another disappointment with a man I cared about. I thought our relationship was going to go in one direction and clearly, I was wrong. When I go back and reread those journals, I am struck by how often I wrote things such as "Why is this happening to me?" or "I'm never good enough." My number one belief was that things were done to me because I wasn't good enough, smart enough, thin enough, pretty enough, quiet enough, whatever enough. What a lightbulb moment for me. All of my clients go through this assessment with me. We discuss their tendencies, the things that cause their stress reactions and begin to discuss strategies to change. This helps them see that they have narratives and stories in their mind that are not truth. They are stories, created by all the conditioning we are exposed to. Conditioning comes from society, community, family, religion, school, etc.

The amount of coaching that happens in the program really helped me to grow. I remember a good friend once saying to me, "I have always loved you. I love this Suzy the best." I was softer. I was happier. I was no longer wound so tight like a top that was about to fly off the table. I was more relaxed. Most of all, I didn't see everything as a problem or negative, I started seeing the world more through the lens of love and compassion. That wasn't the end of my evolution, it was really just the beginning. I projected so much of my hurt, my wounds, my insecurities and my fears that I was not always my best version. In fact, there are times when I look back at something I did or said, and I cringe. I didn't always like the version of me that showed up. I rarely loved the version of me that showed up.

I would hold things in and then at some point lash out. I would take things personally all of the time. I remember one time being in my first condo that my first husband and I purchased. We were having a party and had a large group over. My college roommates who were some of my best friends were there along with other friends from where we lived. Something dropped on the floor and rolled under the range. We all went down on our knees to look under the range, and of course it was gross. The little tomato that dropped was there along with dirt and dust and crumbs. Everyone laughed and I actually got a bit upset. My one friend looked at me later and asked why I got so upset, she hadn't seen me that way before. I told her I felt judged by everyone laughing and was embarrassed. She looked at me and said, "Nobody was laughing at you, everyone was just having fun. We all have stuff under our ranges." That isn't how it felt. It's because I was judging myself. It was because I compared myself to everyone, and I was never good enough. And I was embarrassed, something that only brought shame to me for so long. It was a pattern I didn't realize or break for decades.

Those versions of myself brought me to today. I was different then. I held back voicing how I felt about what people said to me or how they saw me, until I couldn't take it any longer and then I would blow up. I jumped in to help everyone, mostly out of love and loyalty and sometimes out of fear that if I didn't they would no longer love me or want me around. Every relationship seemed tenuous to me. I am sure the fact that I had friends over the years who I lost for various reasons, didn't help those thoughts. It felt like I was on thin ice almost all of the time. Coaching and meditation really enabled me to change a lot of my reactions and mindset. I still found though, that my anger was front and center. That anger, masking intense sadness, was what I no longer wanted to feel. I didn't like how I felt and how easy it could be for me to blow up at someone who questioned me.

One day, I noticed a friend's Facebook post. She basically shared that she had worked to create an entirely new belief structure. That struck a chord. Belief structure? I needed to know more. I saw her the following day at the gym we both worked out at and asked her about it. She immediately told me all about the Mind Magic™ program. This took what she and I learned at iPEC and added neuroscience, energetics, and somatic work. She said it had changed her and her life. Now I needed to look into it. There was a free five-day program coming up that dipped a toe into Mind Magic™ and I immediately signed up for it. This program gave you bits and pieces of the full program so you could see how effective it could be. It certainly had me thinking and wondering what was driving my conscious mind and subconscious mind. The program also started connecting my mind and body, something that I had been really getting to understand more with yoga, meditation and pilates.

Most of us live from our neck up. We live in our mind. We believe all the thoughts our mind thinks. I remember not really understanding Michael Beckwith's comment, "you are not your mind, you are the one with the mind. You are not your body, you are the one with the body." Now I am starting to get it. Our body stores our emotions. Our body hides our secrets. Our body is where we feel our emotions, however we are conditioned not to feel our emotions. Through breath, we connect to our body and calm it, move it out of fight/flight/freeze/fawn. This program introduced all of this to me in a way that made sense. I decided then to sign up for the six-month coaching program of Mind Magic™.

Mind Magic™ helped me to better understand my core beliefs and taught me how to rewire my brain with a new belief system. First, in coaching school I learned that your thoughts inform your feelings; your feelings inform your action/inaction/behavior which then informs your results. Mind Magic™ helped me to see that the underlying belief is what informs your thoughts. By rewiring your belief system, you can actually change your thoughts. Once you do that, your emotions will change, as will your actions and especially your results. Before the program, given my belief structure heavily depended on 'I am not worthy' or 'I am not good enough,' anything that happened would trigger a negative thought, one that was driven from a place of others being better, I can't do it or I am not supposed to be here. Once that was my thought, my feelings would be something like frustration or anger, perhaps self doubt. That could translate one of two ways. One was to take no action. This was a default for me, going hand in hand with giving up before I even tried. The second was I had to prove others and myself wrong so I would over-effort. Neither were good for me no matter what results I ultimately got. Often I ended up feeling like a victim.

Although our brains have the natural propensity to go negative, the negative bias of the primitive brain, you can rewire it if you change your beliefs. This was groundbreaking for me. I finally was able to explore my belief structure. This is when I started to truly understand that "small t" traumas have a compounding effect on you and drive a lot of your behavior. The "large t" traumas bring up everything that the "small t" traumas carry as well. It also means looking at the conditioning you received. Much of it is similar for all of us. As women, we are conditioned to believe that aging is not good, thin is sexy and desirable, and women should keep their opinions to themselves. Many of us are conditioned to think that getting married and having babies is what we are supposed to do. Women tend to be conditioned in society and in families to take care of others. Make dinner, keep the home, learn to serve. Families have their own conditioning; some of mine was around a strong work ethic being of the utmost importance and to never look a gift horse in the mouth. I was also conditioned that I needed to be a leader, my parents held me responsible for anything I did. When they caught me smoking cigarettes at fifteen years old, they never once asked who taught me. They weren't placing blame anywhere but me. I knew I was responsible for my decisions. I find it interesting that somehow that got turned around internally to mean, "ask a lot of opinions and be sure your decision is the right one according to those opinions." Now, I say to myself, "I am my own approval," and I truly believe it. Talk about full circle. None of the conditioning is actually true for anyone, unless you want it to be. We all believed it. This isn't to blame anyone. It is to understand where things came from. It highlights the stories and narratives that are weaved in our minds and how we connect various innocuous comments into a belief about ourselves.

One of the most important pieces to the healing puzzle is understanding that emotions sit in our bodies until we release them. I saw that throughout my life with my mom and even through some of my own experiences. As a coach and healer, I help my clients learn to feel their emotions in order to heal them, and then we work to release them from our bodies. The number one way our bodies expel toxins and remove emotions is through crying. Crying makes so many of us uncomfortable, as if it isn't a safe way to release emotions. We are conditioned to not like when someone cries and to tell people not to cry. I am a believer that crying helps you more than anything. There is a relief I know I feel after I cry. One spot that makes crying easier, safer and all ours, is crying in the shower. The shower gives us permission to be vulnerable with ourselves. We are alone in our nakedness with warm streams of water falling all around us. It is the place to be free to feel all you need to feel without any judgment. There are many ways to release emotions from our bodies:

- Shaking all over
- Crying
- Dancing
- Tapping or EFT
- Primal Screams
- Helicopter Arms
- Massages
- Grounding exercises
- Breathwork
- Oming
- Self-given orgasms

These are just a few of the ways I work with my clients and myself to release the emotions that are pent up. My reflections and exercises that I have shared in this book were developed over the course of time; you cannot rush healing work. I still learn lessons along the way, reflecting on my behavior, others' behavior, and impacts.

While I was writing this book, there were some things that popped up and allowed me a deeper sense of understanding and reflection. One of those was my mom's deep fears. I always knew my mom had poor body image and poor self-esteem. What became clear to me as I was writing was that all of that really stemmed from fear; fear of being authentic and not loved; fear of being alone in the world; fear of rejection; fear of judgment; fear of being less than. My mom went to extremes to protect herself from being hurt, or being seen. In fact, one of the most telling stories about my mom's fears came up as I was talking to my editor.

It was late July in 1995 and my brothers, cousins and I pulled off a surprise seventieth birthday party for our mom, dad and aunt. They were all celebrating this milestone birthday with Dad in July and Mom and Aunt Kit in August. My mom was a twin, fraternal, however they looked a lot alike. There are some photos when they were younger where it is hard to tell them apart. They were all very surprised by the party and seemed happy to see all of their friends and family. A few weeks later, my mom's side of the family held their annual family picnic. We were at a park in Westchester County, New York. My sisters-in-law and I were sitting with a group of our cousins and telling them all about the party.

"We were told it was an anniversary party not a birthday party," said one of my cousins. My two sisters-in-law and I just looked weirdly at each other, not understanding why anyone would say it was an anniversary party. When my mother saw that we were looking at pictures, she ripped them out of our hands and walked away. Everyone was quiet. I looked at the two of them confused.

"I will see what I can figure out," I reassured them. It was obvious my mom would not talk about it and neither would my aunt. A week or so later, I called the cousin who I knew was the keeper of all the documents of our family. As an immigrant Jewish family, the children of my great-grandmother decided to incorporate us into a family circle. It allowed for a family cemetery plot, and ensured that we stayed close to each other. The Francis Spiro Family Circle is why I have second and third cousins who I am as close to as most people are to first cousins.

"Wayne, I need some help."

"Ok, what are you looking for?" he responded.

"I'm not sure. I can't figure out why my mom was so angry and why people thought we threw an anniversary party."

"Do you want to know?"

"Of course," I responded.

He proceeded to share with me that my mom's real birthday was not August 30th, 1925, but was actually May 6th, 1922. They were not twins. He gave me names I had never heard either, Ida and Mildred. Ida, my mom, changed her name to Honey, as my Aunt changed from Mildred to Kit. You could have knocked me over with a feather. For thirty-four years of my life, I thought twins ran in my family, and that perhaps one of us would have twins. For three decades I had been celebrating my mom in August. For longer, Aunt Kit was "sharing" her birthday with mom.

This gnawed at me for a while. All I shared with my sisters-in-law was that they weren't twins. I told them I would get more information. I went to visit my aunt. Of course, she was an accomplice to the lie and I'm sure was sworn to secrecy. I didn't want her to break her oath. I wasn't trying to find this out to hurt anyone. I wanted to know who my mom was, and what happened. I knew my parents really fell for each other the night they met. My dad always told me about how he walked into the Zulu bar in Asbury Park, newly back from the war. He looked across the room and saw the beautiful platinum blonde and knew he needed to meet her.

"I'm going to tell you a story, you can tell me if I am right or wrong," I said to my aunt. "My mom met my dad and realized he was younger than her. She decided to lie about her age and became a twin so that he didn't know she was older." She looked at me with wide eyes, it was obvious I was right and she was not supposed to say anything. That was all I needed. I did ask if my dad knew, and she said she didn't think so. She did share that her husband, my Uncle Tony, knew.

I never told my dad and I didn't let Mom know that I knew for quite a few years. It wasn't my story to tell. My brothers may or may not have been told, I never asked. Life continued on, although a little nuanced. May 6th was Willie Mays' birthday, my all time favorite baseball player, and also my mom's favorite. Every year I would call her on May 6th and say, "Happy birthday, Willie Mays!" It was my way of honoring her day without her knowing I was doing so. For her eightieth birthday, I planned a three-day get away in Atlantic City with Mom and Aunt Kit. I told mom it was for Mother's Day. After I told my mom my big dark secret, that I had an abortion, she shared hers with me. I let her know I knew already. She told me she was afraid to tell my dad, she believed that he would leave her. I looked at her tenderly.

"He loves you and you have been married for sixty years, he isn't going to leave." She was so sure he would. One evening, my brother called me. My dad was going to be turning ninety and would have to begin to take withdrawals from his annuity. My brother called me after he spoke to my dad.

"Suzy, we have a dilemma."

"What is it Jeff?"

" Dad isn't sure which birthday Mom put on the documents."

"He knows?"

"Knows what?"

"You really don't know Jeff."

"You all talk but I don't listen," he said. I laughed, that was true. Then I told him. I called my father immediately.

"You know about Mommy's birthday?"

"You know?" he replied.

"Yes, how did you find out, Dad?"

"When I went to the social security office to start getting my payments, I told them to start Mom's too. They told me I had the wrong birth date." I realized then, he knew since he was in his sixties and never told her.

"Why didn't you say something to her then?"

"I didn't want to hurt her, that was her issue. I didn't care."

"Well Dad, she thinks if you find out you are going to leave her." He decided then he would say something to her so she knew it was okay. We had some very fun moments after this where we were able to joke about this, but it has always stuck with me how fear must have been in my mom's bones for her to keep up that lie for so long, and it was in my bones for a long time, too. My dad's love for my mom was beautiful. To me, this was his greatest testament of that love, to not want to hurt her even after she deceived him. It also showed me how this was my mom's issue and not my dad's.

Looking back, I can really see my mom's insecurities and fears and how those were projected onto me. She was driven by fears; fear of rejection, fear of not being loved, fear of being judged. Her conditioning became my conditioning. Mom had a lot of shame and I did as well. She also taught me the energy of secrets. And it all taught me to stay small, to not be who I could have been, be who everyone wants you to be.Yet, she wanted me to be something special and she pushed me that way. She wanted me to be everything she didn't think she was.

Shame is something that most women carry. And shame keeps us small and hidden as we are ashamed of our shame. Shining a light on our shame disintegrates it. Acknowledging it and helping yourself feel something other than shame is the way to lift that veil. For me, telling my mom about my abortion helped lift that veil of shame. Sharing honest conversations about things I have done helps to lift the veil. No longer being addicted to feeling shame or being the victim and finally allowing myself to love all parts of me without the notion of being perfect, has lifted that veil fully. My little girl is quite happy these days, she no longer feels the shame and embarrassment she once did. She no longer feels lost, rejected or confused. She is fully loved and accepted in a way she never did before. A practice you can try when you realize what you feel shame for is this:

Sit quietly and breathe deeply. I like to have my hand on my heart as I do this. Acknowledge the shame and then let it know you no longer feel shame about whatever. Talk to your shame, let it know you are safe now and allow it to dissipate. Once you acknowledge it, it loses power.

I was always aware I was different; different from members of my family and many of my friends. I felt things way more deeply than anybody around me. My tears came easily, I truly was hurt easily. My mom once told me that I needed to be very careful not to expect other people to have the heart that I had. She was always concerned that I would be hurt a lot in my life because I would expect people to care as much as I did. I don't think I ever truly understood that until my second divorce. I remember feeling like I was such a failure and was at rock bottom. My second husband's last words to me hit hard. He said, "I promised her a better life, and I know that you will be fine." *Wow. I will be fine? Really?* I was swimming in self-doubt, and thought I must be a horrible person. I was completely embarrassed that my marriage blew up the way it did. Having someone say, "You must be hard to live with," just validated everything I was feeling.

What I now know is that I have always been a person who can feel deeply, and this is a very messy world. I tried to hide my depth behind sarcasm, self-deprecating humor, being big and loud, taking up a lot of space. But I felt every single thing that was said to me or action that was taken, and it always felt like a gut punch. What I also now know, is that my deep feelings are what make me, *me*! My deep feelings help me empathize with others and really work to see the situation from their perspective, not mine. My deep feelings allow me to hold so much space for people to feel whatever they need to feel. My deep feelings are what I love about me the most. My deep feelings by themselves would not have been the issue for me had I not had all the self-doubt and self-loathing. They became a part of what I loathed about me. To try to hide my hurt, I used my anger. My anger and fighting for myself was front and center, in my marriages and in some of my friendships.

I have come to realize that the versions of me who were married, were so wounded that I wasn't a good partner either. I grasped too tightly, wanted things the way I wanted them. I fought hard and pushed my spouses away. Whenever I thought we were slipping as a couple, I grasped harder. I fought more. I wasn't the kind and generous partner I thought I was. One of the greatest gifts my healing has brought me has been connecting to and trusting my intuition. Realizing that I knew energetically that my marriage shifted, yet believing him telling me that was just in my head. Realizing that I knew energetically many things in my life, and yet believed what I was told, things I longed to hear. My lack of self love allowed me to disconnect from my own wisdom.

I have done a lot of work to heal, grow and transform from someone who was stuck in self-loathing, a cycle of shame/blame/guilt and a focus on 'should haves' to a woman who is fully expressed, confident in her choices and loves every part of herself no matter who she is today. I wake up each morning and I ask myself, how can I be a better version of me today, than I was yesterday? Some days, that is a slam dunk, the version of me that showed up yesterday sucked. And some days, I'm amazed at what a beautiful, loving human being I am, and I am amazed at how I can be even better.

Healing journeys are not pretty. They don't always feel great, either. In order to truly heal, I have found that you need a few steps. You need awareness of yourself, how you show up, how you act, behave, when you don't act; you have to become really honest with yourself and become truly aware. In order to become truly aware and honest, you need to lose your judgment. All judgment is self projected issues that you have not healed, not looked at fully, not admitted, not even known about. In order to lose your judgment and be honest with yourself, you need grace and space. Grace is giving yourself compassion. Release those perfectionist standards and love yourself without conditions. Space, as in stop being so damn busy. Rest, be, sit in stillness and let the noise begin to subside. As it does, you will begin to hear your inner voice, your inner wisdom.

For me, this journey has taken decades. I have had fits and starts all along the way, allowing things outside of me to derail the work I was doing inside. Some of it couldn't be helped. Grief is one of those things that doesn't move aside when you are working on changing yourself. Grief sneaks up and becomes the centerpiece of what you are feeling. Losing my parents less than three years apart really impacted my journey. My mom's death hit me in ways and at times I didn't realize. A few weeks after her death, I told my boss I was going to leave. I worked with him to figure out how and when we would announce my move. I felt a wave of relief I didn't realize was there, waiting to be released.

I knew that I needed to get away from the pressure, the constant feelings of inadequacy, and the culture of the firm that had changed so dramatically; it was no longer fun. The new people hired were nasty, focused very much on their own success and not that of the team or the business, and most of all, didn't like anyone who was at the firm for a long period of time. I remember one new person hired into a role I held for a long time, she would not give me the time of day. I tried to share information with her and her response was, "I don't need any of the history, we are making changes that you wouldn't understand." The day my boss tried to make this person my boss, I knew it was time to leave the company I once loved. If the company thought someone who was proud that many people don't survive her leadership was the right person to lead, it was definitely time for me to retire.

At first, I was filled with anger and self-doubt. Why would they choose her over me? Why would I no longer be considered for a bigger role? At first, all of the healing I had done seemed to be for naught. I was right back where I once was, feeling like a victim, at the mercy of everyone else. As I distanced myself from my job and started the coaching school, I realized I wasn't a victim. My retirement was the right thing at the right time for me. I could care for my dad and handle whatever he needed.

As the healing continued, my feelings of self-loathing and victimhood began to wane. I started to believe in who I was becoming. I began to create a new belief system where I no longer needed validation from others; where I was my own approval. I began to really trust myself and my intuition. I didn't need others to tell me I was right or wrong. I no longer even looked at things in such a black and white way. Living life without feeling all of your emotions doesn't really feel like living. Allowing myself to finally feel everything, not feel shame for feeling how I feel and allowing myself to lovingly process my emotions has been key to my healing. Releasing expectations to be a certain way, either how I have always been or how society wants me to be, has been liberating. No longer living by anyone else's standard has allowed me to truly understand who I am and how I like to approach the world. I now understand that everything is really a choice. How I look at any situation is a choice. I used to be on auto pilot, reacting the same way I always did. Now, no more auto pilot. I feel how I feel and then I choose a better feeling, a new thought, a reframe of the issue. It is a choice each day to live by the three feelings I want most in my life; Love, Joy and Gratitude.

Losing all of the judgment of myself and talking to myself with love and compassion has allowed me to be honest. I can now be honest about what I love about me, and honest about what I want to change. I now have boundaries, I am intentional about who I am, and who I am becoming, and I no longer do things only to please others. I have released the pressure to be perfect, to be someone I no longer need to be. My authenticity is true, my mask is lifted and I finally love me!

FINAL REFLECTIONS

After the first two years of my blog were published in the book, *The Morning Butterfly*, in 2018, I thought that was the end of writing so vulnerably. That wasn't the case. This book has been inside of me for quite a while now. And after all that I have learned, changed, and grown, vulnerability is what is important to me. Vulnerability and honesty. To myself. To you. I have wanted to share my perspective and story and healing path so that you, my gorgeous reader, know that you are not alone in all of your thoughts and feelings. The stories and the narratives can be changed, you can become much more intentional and move toward joy.

I did not expect that all of that old programming, conditioning and "who I used to be" would pop up along the writing trail. It sure did! The first time I read the book fully I told both my editor and my coach that I thought it sucked. It felt heavy, dark, and I kept wondering, *where the heck was my joy?* My sense of humor was absent. I have had a great life to date and I love where I am today.

I wanted to rewrite the entire thing. I compared myself to others who were writing and those who came before me. I wanted to remove stories, and change order. I struggled to see how anyone would be inspired by anything that I wrote. My runaway thoughts began. *Who am I to write this? Nobody cares about the shit you went through and how you responded. I have been fooling myself into believing I was a writer. I am no writer, I am not even a great coach!*

Fear. I was in the grip of fear. I started to use some of the tools I have. The first one was permission. Permission to not hit the self imposed deadlines. Permission to take time to really feel all of my feelings. Permission to allow myself to re-read it from the perspective of who I was all those years ago, when this book would have helped me. It would have helped me to not feel alone and realize others out there have these thoughts and feelings.

Even though I have spent so many years healing, growing, and transforming, I still get sucked back into that conditioning sometimes. I have found that healing is continual, as is expansion and growth. I still, from time to time, find I am judging myself harshly. As my coach Allyson reminds me, I am so very hard on myself. And although I am softer now, when this pressure comes, I can be pulled back. I could and did get sucked into the pressure instead of moving towards joy. The healing continues. We learn that we haven't completely rewired or dealt with an issue, or we get to learn a deeper truth, a deeper meaning to an old story.

The difference today is I don't stay there. I feel what I have to feel, release it all and take intentional steps towards joy. I bounce back from that fear response quickly. Using all the tools I have, all the knowledge I share, I am able to dance with my fear, regulate my nervous system and move toward joy with a skip in my step.

Each day, after I meditate, I state the Five Principles of Reiki. Reiki is a healing modality using energy and specifically healing hands with life force energy. As a practitioner or master, you are given the energy to use on yourself or others. I am currently a practitioner and looking forward to reaching master.

The Five Principles are:

Just for today, I release angry thoughts. It's normal to feel angry sometimes.
Just for today, I release thoughts of worry.
Just for today, I'm grateful.
Just for today, I expand my consciousness.
Just for today, I'm gentle with all beings.

Stating this helps remind me to be present, to release the anger and worry and be grateful.

I am so grateful for you, beautiful soul. You picked up this book and have made it to the end of my story. I hope it inspires you to begin to rewrite yours. I believe in you and am here to support you. If you would like to go deeper and connect with me, let's set up a connection call and chat. I would love to hear how the book resonated.

With love,
Suzy

Made in the USA
Columbia, SC
22 July 2025

bb796728-897b-46e6-96bf-7bd7fb72531cR01